The Wise Men of Chelm

the wise men of chelm

BY SAMUEL TENENBAUM

Illustrated by Zevi Blum

COLLIER BOOKS
A Division of Macmillan Publishing Co., Inc.
New York

COLLIER MACMILLAN PUBLISHERS
London

Library of Congress Catalog Card Number. 65:18580

FIRST COLLIER BOOKS EDITION 1969
Third Printing 1979

The Wise Men of Chelm was originally published
in a hardcover edition by Thomas Yoseloff, Publisher,
and is reprinted by arrangement.

Macmillan Publishing Co., Inc.
866 Third Avenue, New York, N.Y. 10022
Collier Macmillan Canada, Ltd.

Printed in the United States of America

To Schmuel, from whom in my youth
I learned to love Chelm stories
and who could tell a Chelm story better
than any other person I have ever heard.

Contents

Contents

Preface

CHELM IS A LEGENDARY TOWN, whose inhabitants are known all over the world for their stupidity. Of course, they never suspect this. If truth be told, they rather pity anyone living outside their own town, for other people never do anything in the same way they do. Naturally, if anyone does anything different from them, the other way is the wrong way.

From childhood, I heard about these good, well-meaning—but, oh, such stupid!—Chelmites. When I grew up, I told these stories to children and grown-ups who had not allowed the passing years to dull their sense of humor for the odd and the fanciful. I discovered that they enjoyed hearing these stories about Chelm as much as I had. So I decided to write them down, so that you too may learn to love them and to laugh at these stories as we have.

I know that many persons think of Chelm as a town that once was, fixed and frozen in time, and Chelmites as people who lived in a dead and bygone past. How misinformed they are! For them, it should be said that Chelm is the center of a living, thriving community. Is it possible to have a world without a Chelm? If Chelm perished—forefend the thought!—I have the feeling that we would need right away, as of now, immediately to create another Chelm. If, as we know, Chelm exists, then life goes on there; and if it does, then Chelm stories go on and will go on, and I hope flourish, as long as man loves the odd, the whimsical, the fanciful.

For this reason I have taken the liberty of widening the scope of the Chelm story, and I have placed stories in this collection that may be outside the old, traditional Chelm story. When I encountered a story that had the same genre, the same mood, the same feel of a Chelm story, I included it. For some stories, I had to debate with myself hard and long as to whether they properly belonged. Since they are in the volume, the decision is there for the reading.

In some instances, I have taken a Chelm story and developed it in my own way; in others, I have used only the idea and added considerable material of my own; and in still others, I have created my own Chelm story.

It is difficult to give credit for what I borrowed. I have grown up with many of these stories and they are part of me. Some of the old, traditional Chelm stories are part of folklore and their versions differ with each story teller.

It is my hope you will enjoy these Chelm stories, love them, recall them, and tell them with the same pleasure that I do, for then these tales will be as much yours as mine.

It gives me a peculiar sort of satisfaction to know that this book is being illustrated by Mr. Zevi Blum, whose father, Schmuel, told me Chelm stories when I was very young and from whom I learned to love them. I wish his father were alive to see this book in print. I know that the knowledge of his son's part in this volume would have given him enormous pleasure.

The Wise Men
of Chelm

Chelm Buys a Cow—
and What a Cow!

LEADING AN OLD and broken-down cow by a rope, a stranger wandered into Chelm. He knocked on each door and asked: "Have you a place for me to sleep?"

They all turned him away. Usually the people were kind to strangers, but lately they were very much annoyed and displeased at what other people were saying about them.

"If we are foolish and stupid, why do you come to us?" they asked. On saying that, they closed the door in his face.

After a long search the stranger came to the last house on the street. He knocked on the door. "Can you put me up for the night?" he asked.

The woman of the house half-opened the door, looked at the stranger, and in a severe tone said, "No," and then she hastily shut the door.

It was late at night and the stranger had no place to sleep. Not knowing where to go, he tied his cow to a post on the road and lay down nearby to sleep. The stranger had several gold coins in his pocket. One of his pockets had a hole, and through it several of the gold coins dropped out and rolled near his cow.

A man walked by.

"My! My! Gold coins!" he said, his eyes popping furiously with surprise.

Another man walked by. "What beautiful gold coins!" he exclaimed.

A third man walked by. "Did you ever see the like of it—a cow and gold coins!"

"From where could those gold coins have come?" asked a fourth.

A considerable crowd had collected by now. Everyone wanted to know from where the gold had come.

They examined the ground carefully.

"Certainly," they agreed, "the coins could not come from the stranger. They are quite a distance away from him."

"It is as clear as daylight," said Mr. Bigwig, an important-looking man, rather stout, with a high silk hat. "This cow is different from all other cows. Look how scrawny and thin she is. Could any ordinary cow live who had so many bones showing? But this is an extraordinary cow. It gives out gold coins instead of milk."

Everyone respected Mr. Bigwig, and no one would dare to contradict him, especially when he wore a high silk hat.

"Oooh," said the crowd, very impressed, gasping with the wonder of it all. "A gold-giving cow!"

The story spread quickly, and it grew ever more wonderful in the telling, as each person passed it on to the next.

"I myself saw how a whole torrent of gold coins came out of that rickety cow, flowing as fast as water running over a fall," said one with a big imagination.

"Yes, and it gives nothing less than $100 gold pieces. It does not bother with $5.00 gold pieces, or $10.00 gold pieces, or $25.00 gold pieces," said a second.

"That is true," said a third. "If you so much as show her a penny, a nickel, or a dime, she switches her tail and throws up her hind legs as if she were insulted."

"My! How wonderful!" said the people, their mouths wide open in amazement.

When the stranger awoke in the morning, he found a large and curious crowd surrounding him. They were all anxious to buy his cow. Everyone thought that with a cow like that he could milk out fortunes of money.

"I'll give you $100 for your cow," said a stout man, a prosperous merchant, to the stranger.

"I'll give you $200," said a workman, offering all the money he had saved by a lifetime of hard work.

The stranger could not understand how anyone could be so foolish as to want to give him all that money for his old cow, which gave hardly any milk. He would have been glad to sell her for a few dollars, if he were lucky enough to find someone willing to buy her.

That was why he turned his head in bewildered fashion.

The people thought that he was saying, "No! No!"

"I'll give you $300," said the merchant.

This made the stranger more dazed than ever, and he kept on turning his head this way and that way.

"I'll give you $500 for your cow," said the owner of a large factory.

The more money that was offered for the cow, the less he was able to understand what was happening, and he turned his head from one person to another, amazed at what he was hearing.

This made the people think he was saying, "No! No!"

"She must be a wonderful cow, if he refuses such great sums of money for her," whispered the people in a low voice, so that the stranger could not hear. "She must give out a fortune of money each day. None of us can buy such a cow by himself. Let us assemble all our gold and jewelry, and in this way we may have enough money to buy her."

The people ran to the bank to take out all the money they had. The rich people not only took out all their money, but they also went home and brought back their jewelry and silverware.

All this fortune they piled up in front of the stranger and said: "Will you take this for your cow?"

The stranger couldn't believe his eyes. He pinched himself to make sure that he was awake.

He couldn't believe that his good fortune was real. He was so excited that he could hardly talk.

The people for a moment were afraid that he would refuse the offer. They waited impatiently.

Finally, the stranger stammered in his bewilderment, "I'll sell the cow."

The stranger loaded the jewelry and the money in a truck and rode away.

The people of Chelm rejoiced. With a cow from which poured gold all would be rich. They sang and they danced. No longer would there be any poor people. The children were given a holiday from school. Everyone would now have servants, big houses—everything that they could possibly want.

They approached the cow with care, like a great treasure should be approached. Only one person, the Mayor, was allowed to lead her. The others followed worshipfully at a distance. They took the cow—not to pasture in a field of grass—but to a jewelry store, where precious and valuable objects were kept. They watched her every move lest they do somthing to displease her. Instead of a bucket, they prepared a large jewelry box, which they lined with the most expensive blue velvet. In this they intended to milk the treasure that they were sure would come from the cow. They could hardly wait for milking time. At sundown, the town officials, dressed in their holiday clothes, gathered around the cow. Before they touched her, an elaborate ceremony was held. Nothing was left undone, as you notice, to show the cow the respect in which she was held.

Finally, the Mayor, with his own hands, began to

milk. With great care the town officials held up the jewelry box.

The town now waited for the flood of gold to start pouring forth.

The Mayor squeezed the teats of the cow. There came forth, not gold, but milk. Again he squeezed, and more milk came out, and not even good milk but watery milk.

"The cow is playing a joke on us," said the people, not willing to believe that they had been fooled.

"Maybe the coins are in the milk," said a high official.

The mayor examined the milk and found—only milk.

The faces of the people became white and pale. They began to tremble. They had parted with all their money for a worthless cow. Now they were penniless.

"We have been cheated!"

"We have been ruined!"

"If we find that man who sold us the cow we shall scold him severely."

Thus they cried.

The Wise Men of Chelm who were present stepped forward.

"We believe," they said, calmly, "that you are doing an injustice to an innocent man. What one sees with his own eyes one must believe. All of us saw the gold right near the cow. Where else could it have come from but from the cow?"

"What shall we do now?" asked the people.

"We shall have to think," said the Wise Men. "Since all this has happened so unexpectedly, we shall think right here in the jewelry store and not in our skyscraper. Although we haven't our regular meeting place, we shall think wisely."

The people held their breath while the Wise Men thought. After many hours, one of the Wise Men stroked his beard and said: "We must find the man who sold us the cow. Perhaps we do not know how to milk her. He will be able to tell us what is the matter."

"That is right," said the people, feeling much better. The color came back to their cheeks. They began to smile a little.

"Do not worry," said the Wise Men. "We shall send Mr. Temperless"—he was the owner of the town's department store—"to search for the stranger in neighboring towns. When we find him, all will be well."

The people, much relieved, departed for their homes. Certain again that they had bought a great treasure, they went about their business as always. While Mr. Temperless was looking for the stranger, the Wise Men took care of the cow. The town wouldn't for a moment have the cow associate with ordinary people.

After several weeks of searching, Mr. Temperless found the stranger living in a mansion with many servants.

"When we milked the cow, nothing came out," said Mr. Temperless to the stranger when he saw him.

The stranger did not understand.

"Not even an ounce of gold came out," said Mr. Temperless, by now excited.

"Gold?" asked the stranger.

Now everything was clear to him.

"So these people thought that gold came out of my broken-down cow?" he thought, hardly able to keep from laughing. "Have you fed the cow?" he asked, in a very serious voice.

"What do you mean 'fed the cow'?" asked Mr. Temperless.

"I mean, have you given the cow anything to eat?"

Mr. Temperless did not know what to answer. He hemmed and hawed. "I suppose so, but I don't know," stammered Mr. Temperless.

"Well," said the stranger, who wasn't a very honest man, "that may be the trouble. The cow which you bought is peculiar. Unlike other cows, it was trained not to eat. It took a long time to train her, but when I owned her, she was able to get along without food. That's the only time when the cow can give out gold."

"What shall we do if we have fed the cow?" asked Mr. Temperless.

"Then she has lost all her valuable training. She can give only milk. You must then train her all over again to live without food. As soon as you succeed, she will begin to give gold."

"Oh! I see," said Mr. Temperless.

He hastened back to Chelm and sought out the Wise Men.

"That stranger," he said to the Wise Men, "is as honest as water is wet."

"Yes, yes," said the Wise Men, eager to hear his story.

"Have you fed the cow?"

"Certainly," said the Wise Men, aggrieved that

anyone should think that they could forget such a thing. "You must not ask us such foolish questions. Even our two fools know that a cow must be fed."

"You have made a serious mistake," said Mr. Temperless, becoming pale.

"Why?" said the Wise Men, wondering why Mr. Temperless appeared so miserable. "We have given the cow the best hay we could find. We have given her the finest cake and desserts that our baker could make. No cow has ever been better treated."

"There lies the trouble," said Mr. Temperless.

"Where's the trouble?" asked the Wise Men.

"That cow should not have touched food. She was trained not to eat. What you must do now is to make her dislike food."

Mr. Temperless then related his conversation with the stranger.

"If we stop feeding her now," said the Wise Men, "she will die. We shall have to train her gradually, until she gets into the habit of not eating."

The Wise Men gave the cow less and less to eat every day.

At the end of a month, the cow was given only a half-ounce of straw every two days. The cow had become thin and scrawny, but the people did not notice that.

"Tomorrow," said the Wise Men, "we shall give the cow nothing to eat, and then we shall have lots of gold, as much gold as we want."

The next day the town officials and the people put on their best clothes. Everyone was again happy. Chelm would be the richest town in the world! What a treasure they had bought! They would have servants and mansions and everything they wanted!

They gathered in front of the jewelry store. When they were all assembled, they went in.

They had no chance to milk the cow.

The cow was dead.

The people grieved and mourned.

"Was the cow fair? Was the cow honest?" they complained. "Just as soon as we have her trained, she dies. What can you do with a mean cow like that?"

"That is true," said the Wise Men. "If that cow could have managed to live only one more day, all would have been well. As soon as we had the cow almost trained, she died."

That taught the people of Chelm a lesson. They would never buy any more gold cows. Buying a goat, however, that gave gold, or a chicken that laid golden eggs, was an altogether different matter.

Ruined by a Pair of Shoelaces

MR. DINKLE, a wealthy merchant of Chelm, was taking a walk down Main Street one Saturday afternoon. He felt one of his shoes suddenly becoming loose. A little later the shoe slipped from his foot.

"My, my," he said to himself, "my shoelace has ripped. I shall have to buy a new pair."

He bought a new pair of shoelaces and continued walking.

He was not comfortable, however. He kept looking at his shoelaces and then at his shoes. "People must be staring at me," he thought. "I must present a funny appearance wearing such new shoelaces and such old shoes. It doesn't look right for a person in my position to be seen like this."

He walked into a shoestore and bought a fine pair of shoes to match his fine shoelaces.

"This is better," he said, as he kept on walking.

But soon he was again uncomfortable. He looked at his new shoes and then at his overcoat. "People must be staring at me," he thought. "It is indeed queer to wear such fine shoes and such a shabby overcoat."

He came to a clothing store and there bought a fine overcoat to match his fine shoes and fine shoe-laces.

"This is much better," he said, as he kept on walking.

Soon he was again uncomfortable. "People must be staring at me," he thought. "It's a disgrace for a person like me to wear such a fine pair of shoes, such a beautiful overcoat, and such an old, thread-bare suit."

He then went into another clothing store and bought a new suit to match his new shoelaces, his new shoes, and his new overcoat.

"This is much better," he said to himself, as he kept on walking.

Soon he was so uncomfortable that he turned off Main Street into a side street where no one could see him. He was afraid that someone would laugh at him.

"It would serve me right," he thought. "I must look silly wearing so fine an overcoat, so beautiful a suit, so good a pair of shoes, so new a pair of shoelaces, and such an old, dirty-looking hat."

He felt so ashamed of himself that he walked into a store and bought a new hat to match his other clothing.

Proudly, and in high spirits, he walked on Main Street. He wished that all his friends could see him.

When through with his walk, he returned home. His dog did not recognize him and began to bark, as if a stranger had entered the gate. Mr. Dinkle crawled into his own house through the back entrance.

"Another tramp is probably trying to beg a meal," thought his wife, as she noticed someone prowling outside.

When she got a look at the man who was coming in, she thought: "Unlike other tramps, he is richly dressed, better dressed than our banker. Such a man does not deserve help."

She became angry and picked up a broom and was about to bring it down on Mr. Dinkle's head.

"Get out quickly," she shouted. "You look altogether too prosperous to go around begging."

"My dear wife," said Mr. Dinkle, "I am your husband."

At first the wife refused to believe it, but after examining him more closely, she did indeed recognize him.

"My! How you have changed!" she said in astonishment. "Even your own wife doesn't know you! What new clothes you have! You look handsome."

Mr. Dinkle proudly showed all the clothes he had bought.

His wife grabbed the broom and again was about to bring it down on his head.

"What is the matter now, dear wife?" he asked, alarmed.

"How does it look," she said, "for a husband to be so beautifully dressed and for his wife to be so poorly dressed? I shall be ashamed to go with you among people. They will not believe I am your

27

wife. They will think I am a poor relative. You must go out with me immediately and buy me new clothes to match yours."

Then and there they went out and, when they returned, Mrs. Dinkle was as splendidly dressed as her husband.

As they were about to go into their house, the husband said: "How does it look for two people as well dressed as we are to live in such a small house? It will never do. Everybody will laugh at us."

So Mr. and Mrs. Dinkle bought a new house with many, many rooms.

When they were about to move their furniture from their old house to their new one, both Mr. and Mrs. Dinkle said: "It doesn't look right to live in such a big, fine house and to have such old furniture."

They threw their old furniture away and bought new furniture to match their house.

By this time, Mr. Dinkle had spent, not only his own money, but all the money he could borrow. He was in great debt. The people to whom he owed money wanted it returned, but Mr. Dinkle had no money with which to pay back. His debtors, therefore, took away his house, his furniture, his clothes and everything he had.

Mr. and Mrs. Dinkle had nothing new—not even new shoelaces. Since everything they now had was old and shabby, they were content.

A Duck and a Drake

"How can you recognize the difference between a he-duck and a she-duck?" asked a child in Chelm of his teacher.

The teacher thought and thought and finally said: "You can recognize the difference in this way. Throw the two birds a piece of bread. If she catches it first, then it is a duck. If he catches it first, then it is a drake."

"That's very simple," said the children in the class, as they nodded their heads, as if to say, "It's too easy, too easy."

Chelm's Sexton

FOR MORE THAN FIFTY YEARS the Sexton of Chelm had called the faithful to worship. He had never failed in his duty a single day. On holiday mornings he knocked on the shutters of each house with his heavy cane and called out in his piercing voice: "Time for worship! Time for worship!" Even the oldest inhabitant could not remember when their good, faithful Sexton hadn't done this.

Now he was old and feeble. Instead of walking briskly he hobbled. His loud voice had become faint and cracked. The good people of Chelm felt badly that such an old and good man had to be out so early in the morning when most of the town was still asleep.

"An old man like him should rest more," said one.

"He may become sick," said another.

Thus did they sympathize with him, but they did nothing to help him. As always, they waited in their warm beds until the Sexton summoned them to services. None of them went without being called.

One holiday morning the rabbi of Chelm was surprised to find the pews not filled, but half-empty. This had never happened before. He started the service, however. The parishoners kept on arriving, acting as if they weren't really late. In fact, they seemed to be angry when they noticed that the service was almost over.

Unable to continue the services because of the disturbance, the rabbi scoldingly said: "What is happening to our beloved town? Have we become lax and sinful? For the first time many of you have come late for services. Others haven't come at all. This is shocking!"

There was quiet as he spoke, but the silence was interrupted by Mrs. Good as Gold, who had never been late or missed services in all her life.

"Our most revered rabbi, it is not our fault that we are late," she said.

With an icy look, the rabbi said: "I suppose it is my fault."

Ashamed and with head bowed, Mrs. Good as Gold humbly explained: "As soon as the Sexton knocked on our shutters we immediately came to services."

"That is so," said Mrs. Almost as Good as Gold, who was also very pious. "My family started out as soon as the Sexton called us, the same as we have done for the last twenty years."

"I understand now," said the rabbi, deeply apologetic. "It is our Sexton who has made you late. It takes him so long to get around. He is not

31

as young as he was fifty years ago. Come to think of it, he is exactly fifty years older now than he was fifty years ago. We must do something to help him."

The people of Chelm went to the Wise Men who thought and thought and thought. Whenever the Wise Men thought, something always happened. This time something happened, too.

One fine morning a horse and wagon drew up in front of each house and two strong men got off, went into each house, and began to remove the shutters.

"What are you doing?" asked the housewives, objecting.

"The Wise Men have ordered us to do this," explained the shutter-removers. That was all that the housewives needed to hear. If the Wise Men wanted something done, that thing couldn't help but be wise and smart.

Soon there wasn't a house in all Chelm that had a shutter on its windows.

The big wagon—which by now was overflowing with shutters piled up high—drove up to the humble house of the Sexton, and the driver carefully deposited all the shutters inside his house.

"What are you doing?" asked the astonished Sexton. "There isn't a place for me to sit or stand. I am practically without a home in my own house."

"The Wise Men and the whole town will assemble at your house tonight and explain matters to you," said the driver.

That night, in the presence of the whole town, one of the Wise Men, stroking his long beard and furrowing his brow deeply, began to explain:

"You, our good Sexton, have been a faithful servant. You have become old and feeble serving us. We feel that you deserve a rest. It is too hard for a man of your years to walk from house to house in all kinds of weather, in the cold, in the rain, and in the snow, and to knock on each of our shutters. So we have gathered all the shutters in your own house. On cold days you will now be able to remain in your warm house, and without going out, knock on all the shutters as you have been doing for the last fifty years. Why should you go out to the shutters when we can bring the shutters to you? It was difficult to think of the idea, but we, the Wise Men of Chelm can think of things which nobody else can."

Saying this, the Wise Man who was speaking patted himself on the shoulder and all the other Wise Men patted each other on the shoulder. And the people were very proud of their Wise Men.

On the next religious holiday, the Sexton, instead of going out, knocked on all the shutters in his own house.

Everybody, including the Sexton, agreed that it was much easier, and it saved a lot of walking. And everybody was sorry that they had not thought of asking the Wise Men to help them a long time before.

The Cobbler of Chelm
Goes Traveling

THE COBBLER OF CHELM was left a fortune by a
relative he had never known or seen. Not once in
his life had he ever been outside the town in which
he lived. He had spent all his days mending shoes.
Now, since he had inherited a fortune, he wanted to
travel. He wanted to see strange places he had
heard about. He wanted to see how other people
lived, how they worked, what clothes they wore;
in short, what they were like.

One morning he harnessed his faithful old horse
to his old wagon. He climbed up to the seat, said
"Giddy-yap," and began riding to the railroad station. When he reached it, he got off the wagon,
said goodbye to his horse, and went inside. He
thought that all he had to do to travel was to wait
in the railroad station. He did not know that he
had to take a train to go anywhere. He sat down

on one of the seats in the station and he thought he was moving.

"Traveling is really wonderful," he said to himself. "Why, it feels just as if I were in my own cobbling shop."

Thus he sat and sat and sat. The longer he sat in the waiting room the more wonderful did traveling appear to him. "Oh! These inventions!" he thought. "They are even greater than I imagined. One wouldn't think that one is moving and yet one is."

After waiting for five hours, he became hungry. "I have ridden far enough," he thought. "I shall now go out, eat in a restaurant, and then see the strange town."

Outside of the railroad station he noticed an old horse hitched to an old wagon. "This horse and buggy look exactly like the horse and buggy I left behind in Chelm. How remarkable!"

He began walking down Main Street. Sure enough, it was exactly like the Main Street he had seen all his life. In fact, some of the passersby called him by name and wanted to talk to him. Since he was in another town, he thought it was foolish to talk to them, as they only thought they knew him.

He came to a street which looked exactly like the one on which was his cobbling shop. Wonder of wonders! Sure enough, there was his cobbling shop! Of course, it wasn't his. He knew that. Wasn't he in a strange town? But he could swear that the shop looked almost like his own.

"Well," he thought, "every town must be like my town, Chelm. All over the world there must be hundreds of towns exactly like Chelm. There must be hundreds of cobbling shops exactly like mine, with hundreds of cobblers exactly like me. All the doctors in all the towns must be exactly like our own Dr. Castor Oil Magnesia. All the farmers, all over the world, must be exactly like our Mr. Sharpy Weiselhead. This is indeed wonderful!"

After he had seen all he wanted, he went back to the railroad station and sat down in the waiting room.

"A railroad is the most remarkable thing in the world," he thought, as he sat and sat and sat. "It doesn't make any difference whether you are going to or returning from a town. The railroad, without being told, knows where to take you."

After waiting in the railroad station five hours—which was exactly the time it took him to leave Chelm—he said to himself: "I must be back now in my own town. I shall go out."

Outside the railroad station he saw the same town which he knew so well. His horse was waiting for him.

"Although this is the first time I have ridden on a railroad, I haven't had any mishaps," he thought, pleased with himself. "I traveled as I wanted and I came back as I wanted. I didn't do badly at all."

Back in his cobbling shop, he was visited by old friends who came to greet him.

"Have you returned?" they asked.

"You can see for yourself that I have," answered the cobbler.

"How is traveling?" they inquired. None of them had ever been outside of Chelm.

"It is wonderful," the cobbler said.

"Have you seen any strange sights?"

"Everything I saw was indeed strange. It reminded me of our own Chelm and yet it wasn't Chelm, which makes it all the more wonderful."

"What are the streets of other towns like?"

"Exactly like ours, only different."

"How are the people?"

"Exactly like ours, only different."

"How are the buildings?"

"Exactly like ours, only different."

Since they could not understand how anything could be exactly the same and yet different, they thought the cobbler must be very smart, and they respected him as they never did before. In fact, they even elected him as one of the Wise Men of Chelm, for they said that he was traveled and could advise the Wise Men on how other towns managed their affairs.

Chelm's Doctor

AFTER ITS WISE MEN, Chelm respected most its doctor. He had been graduated from college and had diplomas, big, beautiful diplomas with ribbons around them. Everyone said that his diplomas were the best possible diplomas, and that therefore he must be the best possible doctor.

His name was Dr. Castor Oil Magnesia, which anyone, even at first glance, could see was a highly appropriate name for a doctor. Dr. Castor Oil Magnesia was short, stout and had two eyes that bulged out like two big yellow pumpkins. They were just the right eyes for a doctor, as they looked serious and frightening, which was the way that doctors' eyes should look. Dr. Magnesia moved slowly, like a turtle, and he was always in a daze. When parents became alarmed about the illness of their children, he would listen gravely and always say, "Quite so. Quite so."

"My child coughs so loudly that the house

trembles," said a nervous mother, whose child had a small cough.

Dr. Castor Oil Magnesia stared through his yellow, pumpkin eyes and said: "What? What?"

"My child coughs so loudly," said the mother, "that our dog thinks another dog is barking and barks back."

"What? What?" said Dr. Castor Oil Magnesia, his owl-like eyes turning around like a pinwheel. He then said what he always said: "Quite so! Quite so!"

The mother now became thoroughly alarmed. "Our child is dying," she wailed, tears streaming down her face.

"Quite so! Quite so!" said Dr. Castor Oil Magnesia.

Of course, the child didn't die. For curing him, Dr. Castor Oil Magnesia was given a great deal of praise. "He snatched my child from death," said the happy mother.

"My son was so sick," said another mother, who liked to make things more serious than they were, "that his feet were thin as spider-webs. He hadn't the strength to talk. He could only shout at the top of his lungs and cough. Our Dr. Castor Oil Magnesia is a wonder."

The news that Dr. Castor Oil Magnesia planned to leave Chelm and study further came as a surprise to everyone. The women said that the whole idea was ridiculous. Nobody could teach Dr. Castor Oil Magnesia anything.

The Wise Men shook their heads, stroked their beards, and disapproved. "Our doctor," they said, "can teach others, but no one can teach our doctor."

To all this, Dr. Magnesia turned his pinwheel eyes furiously and said, "What? What?" and then, "Quite so! Quite so!"; and then he departed for a neighboring town, where he began to study with Dr. Smarty Smarter Smartest.

"I shall let you handle the next case," said Dr. Smarty Smarter Smartest. "I shall observe how you do it."

When they reached the house of the sick man, his wife was greatly upset. "My husband is very sick," she said. "All night he has been in great pain."

"My stomach! My stomach! It is killing me! I am dying!" groaned the sick man.

Because the patient was complaining about his stomach, Dr. Castor Oil Magnesia carefully examined the man's feet, back and ears. That's how he always did things.

"The trouble with you," said Dr. Castor Oil Magnesia, "is that you have tired yourself washing too many floors. You must be careful about the number of floors you wash a day. Never wash more than three hundred."

"I haven't washed a single floor," protested the man. "My wife does that. I am afraid you do not understand my sickness."

"Quite so! Quite so!" said Dr. Castor Oil Magnesia.

"You probably do not understand what Dr. Magnesia says," suggested Dr. Smarty Smarter Smartest. "The doctor probably means that you ate too much canned foods. That gave you a stomach ache."

"Quite so! Quite so!" said Dr. Magnesia.

"That's true," said the sick man. "Lately, my wife

41

has had so much trouble with the children that she hasn't had time to prepare supper, so we have been eating out of cans."

When they were outside, Dr. Smarty Smarter Smartest said scoldingly: "Don't you know that men generally don't wash floors? It's the women who do that."

"How did you know that he ate canned foods?" asked the astonished Dr. Magnesia.

"Simple," said Dr. Smartest. "I noticed outside the house many empty tin cans."

"I understand. I understand," said Dr. Castor Oil Magnesia. "I shall know better next time."

Soon they were called to another sick person.

"My stomach! My stomach!" moaned a small boy who was sick.

"He has been having the most awful pains," said his worried mother.

"Quite so! Quite so!" said Dr. Magnesia.

Because the boy's stomach was paining him, he examined the child's head, nose, throat and arms.

"He ate canned food and that made him sick," said Dr. Magnesia.

"How dare you!" cried the mother, highly indignant. "I wouldn't consider giving him such food. I prepare all the food he eats myself and I choose only the best."

"Quite so! Quite so!" said Dr. Magnesia, blinking his eyes, for he was very much afraid that the angry woman might pound a broom over his head.

"My good woman," said Dr. Smarty Smarter Smartest, sweetly, talking as a doctor should. "Your son ate green apples. Let me ask him if that is not true."

"If he did, I shall give him the thrashing of his life," said the mother, who was a mother with whom a child couldn't misbehave.

At first the boy said that he hadn't eaten green apples, but after awhile he admitted that he had stayed away from school and cleaned out the apple orchard.

When they were outside, the astonished Dr. Magnesia asked: "How did you know what he ate?"

"It was simple," said Dr. Smarty Smarter Smartest. "As we were riding to the house, I noticed in the orchard the cores of many apples."

The next patient they visited was a woman who complained of terrible pains in her back. Because her back was hurting her, Dr. Magnesia carefully examined her stomach.

"Quite so! Quite so!" said Dr. Castor Oil Magnesia.

"What do you mean, 'Quite so! Quite so!'?" asked the woman, who was in great pain and grouchy. She did not understand the doctor as the people in Chelm did.

"You have been chopping wood and have overexerted yourself," Dr. Magnesia explained to the woman.

"What do you mean 'chopping wood'?" cried the woman, in a rage. "My husband attends to that."

"Well, my good woman," said Dr. Smarty Smarter Smartest, interrupting. "What Dr. Castor Oil Magnesia means is that you have bought new furniture."

"That I have," said the woman, pleased. "Isn't this a beautiful bedroom set? And have you noticed my dining room set?"

"Your furniture is indeed beautiful and does

credit to your taste," said Dr. Smarty Smarter Smartest. "You have probably spent many hours arranging the furniture to suit you, taking one piece from one corner and trying it out in another corner."

"That I have done," admitted the woman.

"Now, my good woman, in lifting the heavy pieces you have sprained your back."

"That is right," said the woman. "That is right."

When they returned to Dr. Smartest's office, Dr. Castor Oil Magnesia said: "I have learned a great deal. I understand your method. I am now returning to Chelm. I shall now be able to cure people better than I have ever before. I shall be the best doctor there."

Already, in his mind's eye, he was picturing to himself how proud everyone would be of him. This made his pumpkin eyes twirl and whirl in great glee.

When he reached Chelm, Dr. Castor Oil Magnesia was immediately called to the bedside of a sick man. He put a thermometer into the man's mouth, gravely shook his head, and said: "Bad—very bad."

"But what is the matter?" asked the wife, alarmed.

"Your husband has done something serious, something he should never have done."

"What has he done?" pleaded the wife, wringing her hands in grief.

"He has swallowed a horse," said Dr. Castor Oil Magnesia.

"Swallowed a horse!" exclaimed the wife.

"Swallowed a horse?" asked the sick man, not

understanding. "I have never done anything of the kind," he protested.

"Come my good man," said Dr. Castor Oil Magnesia, "here is the horse's harness right under your bed. And the horse is missing. That's how I know you have swallowed a horse."

"I use the harness to put on the horse when I go out to peddle," the man tried to explain.

This made his wife even more angry. "Not only have you swallowed a horse," she shouted, "but you are contradicting the doctor."

Nobody, as you know, ever contradicted a doctor in Chelm.

"But I haven't swallowed a horse," insisted the sick man.

"Then, why are you sick?" asked the wife.

The husband could not answer. He did not know why he was sick. This proved that the doctor was right.

"If the doctor says you have swallowed a horse," said the woman, "you have swallowed a horse."

Although this was one of Dr. Castor Oil Magnesia's most difficult cases, the sick man, after a long illness, became well. He still insisted that he never swallowed a horse, but the people of Chelm had their own ideas. Those who owned horses were careful to keep them far away from him, for they remembered what Dr. Castor Oil Magnesia said about him.

Chelm Builds
a Town Hall

A STRANGER CAME TO CHELM. He was a little man and a quiet man. And yet when he left, the whole town was in an uproar because of him.

The stranger took one look at the town hall, and said, just as he was leaving, "In Pulpy, where I live, our town hall is nicer, bigger, and better."

"That is impossible," said Mr. Temper, who overheard the remark. "Remember, you are in Chelm and here everything is better, bigger, and smarter."

The stranger did not agree. In fact, he said: "Not only is your town hall not as nice as ours, but it isn't nearly as nice as any of the town halls I visit, and I visit many towns."

Saying that, he jerked his reins, and his horse galloped away.

Mr. Temper repeated the conversation to his

wife, and his wife, who was horrified, quickly told her friends.

Soon, you may be sure, everyone in Chelm had heard of what happened and everyone who heard the story felt badly.

At last they went to the Mayor. They said: "If we in Chelm are the smartest people in the world— and you know we are—we should have the best of everything."

"That is right," said the Mayor, becoming enraged. "All of us have been insulted," he cried.

The bags of flesh around his stomach jumped up and down like jelly. That is what always happened when he was excited. Most of the time, however, he was good-natured and jolly. Now he was unhappy and worried.

"We must do something," he cried, banging his fist on his desk.

"We must do something," cried the people.

But what to do they did not know.

They thought of one thing and then they thought of another thing. It was 8 o'clock; it was 10 o'clock; it was 12 o'clock at night. They were still thinking.

They stayed up so late that many of the people of Chelm became sleepy. Several began to snore right then and there; and, as the hours passed, more and more of them began to snore.

Finally, the noise became so great that they woke each other up.

"How can one sleep when everyone else makes so much noise?" asked one, sleepy-eyed and angry, who himself sounded like a locomotive when asleep.

"You are here to think, not sleep," cried the Mayor, who tried to act as if he were wide awake, but whose eyes were drooping and three-quarters shut.

"Let us go home and think," said a practical-minded woman.

"That is a good idea," they all agreed, having in mind their soft, comfortable beds.

Wearily, they all went home.

When they awoke the next morning, they still remembered the insult. In their unhappiness, they could not eat. They lost pounds and pounds of weight. They began to resemble toothpicks.

The Mayor lost more weight than anyone, but no one cared because he could well afford to lose it. After losing one hundred and fifty pounds, he still weighed two hundred and forty-nine pounds, and he was still the fattest man in all Chelm.

The Mayor became sick and had to be taken to a hospital.

This made him popular with the people. "You see," they said, "how our Mayor takes to heart an insult to our town."

Now something certainly had to be done.

One day the people went in a great crowd to the Wise Men of Chelm and said: "Our Mayor is in the hospital. We cannot stand the thought that our town is behind any other town in anything. We are worrying ourselves sick."

"That is true," said the wives. "Our husbands are becoming so thin that soon we won't be able to see them, which will make us practically widows. What is the use of husbands we cannot see?"

"Our wives," said the husbands, "are becoming

so thin that soon we won't be able to see them without a microscope. What is the use of wives we can only see through a microscope, especially when we haven't a microscope?"

The Wise Men stroked their beards, nodded their heads, and said: "We shall attend to the matter."

The people returned to their homes and the Wise Men sat down to think. They thought and thought.

As their minds worked, the people heard a buzzing and whirring. So great was the noise that some people thought that a terrible monster had descended upon them; others thought that an airplane was soaring over the rooftops. They ran out of their houses. They were relieved when they discovered that the strange sounds were coming from the meeting place of the Wise Men.

"Shhhh!" they said, as they walked on tip-toe. "Our Wise Men—God bless them—are thinking. We must not disturb them."

"This is the most difficult problem that we have ever had to solve," they said. "We have thought so hard that our thinking machinery is in danger of exploding. But thanks to our wisdom . . ." Here the Wise Men puffed out their chests and stroked their beards vigorously. ". . . we have found the answer."

The inhabitants cupped their hands behind their ears and craned their necks forward.

Amid a deep silence, the Wise Men continued: "We have decided to build a new town hall, bigger, better, finer and more beautiful than anything that exists in any neighboring town or, for that matter, in any town. And we—the Wise Men—shall take personal charge of the building, and this should be a guarantee that it will be everything we expect from it."

The people let out a sigh of relief. They would now be able to gain back the weight they had lost. Their Wise Men were indeed smart!

As soon as the Mayor was told of what took place, he jumped out of his hospital bed, a well man.

In a short time, the new town hall was completed. In a body, the town held a parade before the official opening.

The Mayor, now his jovial old self, led the procession.

Directly behind him followed the Wise Men, who walked with great dignity, stroking their beards each time they took a step.

As they came in view of the building, everybody let out an exclamation of delight. Truly, it was beautiful! The front was made of white marble; the steps leading to the entrance were wide and stately. At the top of the stairway was a row of high pillars. The building was immense, about ten blocks long. Never had there been a town hall the equal of it!

The Wise Men stroked their beards vigorously, conscious that the trust placed in them by the town was justified.

"When we Wise Men do something, we do it superbly—and perfectly," one of them was heard to say.

It was decided that the Mayor should enter first.

His fat face was one big smile. "This is the happiest moment of my life," he said.

As he was about to enter the stately building, he could not find a door through which to enter. He examined the building stone for stone, but he could not find a single door. The people examined the building stone by stone, but they could not find a single door.

The town hall had everything—beautiful wide stairways, ornate windows—but it had no door.

The Wise Men had forgotten to build a door.

But that did not trouble the people of Chelm. There and then, they took off their coats and jackets and began to lift the building.

"Quick! Quick!" said the men, straining every muscle to hold up the building while motioning to the Mayor to enter.

Slowly and with great dignity as befits a Mayor, he put his head forward. At this point, the weight became too heavy for the men to hold. The building dropped on top of the Mayor.

All the townspeople in the parade hastened to see what had happened. They found the body of the Mayor outside of the building, but they couldn't find his head.

"How strange!" said the people. "The Mayor has no head."

The Wise Men examined the body carefully, but they also could not find a head. After long deliberation, they took one long stroke on their beards and said in unison: "It is true. The Mayor has no head."

"What could have happened?" asked the people.

The Wise Men thought and thought. As they thought, their minds whirred and churned, as if a cyclone had been let loose.

"The thing to do," they finally said, "is to find the head of the Mayor."

The people scattered in all directions. One went searching down Main Street, thinking that the Mayor might have lost his head there. Another went to the old town hall. Another went to the ice cream parlor. They knew that the Mayor was fond of candy and ice cream. That's how he had become so fat.

But they all came back without the Mayor's head. No one could find it.

"Let us go over to the Mayor's wife," said the Wise Men. "She may know where her husband's head is."

They found her at home. It didn't surprise her in the least that they had the body of the Mayor and not his head. She knew immediately what was the matter.

"Lately—since the trouble about the town hall arose—the Mayor has been going around the house saying, 'I am losing my head! I am losing my head!' I suppose," she said, calmly, "he must have lost it."

Everyone was much relieved by the explanation.

"There is nothing to worry about now," said the Wise Men. "If anything is lost, it will be found. It may take time, but in the end it will be found. All of you should now go home. When you have an idle moment, however, you should search for the Mayor's lost head."

To this day, the people of Chelm, when they have an idle moment, organize searching parties. Neither they nor the Mayor's wife are in the least worried. As they explain: "It's only a matter of time before we shall find the lost head. When we do find it, we shall put it back on the Mayor's body and then he'll be the same as he always was. This should serve him as a good lesson not to be so careless as to lose his head again."

Dr. Pimplewasser
Finds Himself

One of the Wise Men of Chelm was very absent-minded. He always forgot things.

"Ah!" said the people. "Doesn't that show he is truly a wise man? He cannot bother remembering small things, for his mind is full of important matters."

They always delighted in telling stories of their beloved Dr. Pimplewasser, for that was his name.

One of the stories they never tired of telling was what happened when Mrs. Pimplewasser hired a new maid. The doctor had come home late one evening after having delivered a lecture on how to improve one's memory.

As he walked up the steps of his house, he saw underneath the doorbell a sign which read, "Please ring." When he did so, the new maid came out and asked, "Whom did you wish to see?"

"Is Mrs. Pimplewasser at home?" he inquired, not knowing who the woman was.

"No, she is not here," answered the maid.

"Is Dr. Pimplewasser at home?" he asked, bewildered.

"No, he's not here. In truth, no one is at home."

Dr. Pimplewasser stared at the maid for a while, and then walked down the steps, now knowing what to do, or what other questions to ask. He was sure he lived in this house and yet it seemed he didn't.

He went from house to house, asking, "Does Dr. Pimplewasser live here?"

At every house he got the same answer, "No."

He wandered around through the streets for hours, befuddled and unhappy, until by chance he ran into his wife, who took him home with her.

In the morning, when Dr. Pimplewasser awoke, he would shout down to his wife on the floor below: "I, your husband, am in bed, and I do not remember where I put my clothes before going to bed."

This made Mrs. Pimplewasser very angry, for she had been helping her husband find things for many years.

"All your clothes are in your bedroom. Go and find them," she called back to him. "I cannot go up and help you. I am preparing breakfast."

She was good and tired of waiting on him as if he were a child.

Dr. Pimplewasser got out of bed and looked and looked and looked. At last he was all dressed.

Proudly, he went downstairs to the living room.

It was not often he managed to dress without help.

Instead of his wife's praising him, she was more angry than ever.

"What have you been doing until now?" she cried.

"Why, dressing, of course," replied Dr. Pimplewasser. "And you see, my dear, I did it without help."

"Why, why . . ." spluttered his wife, almost speechless. "Do you know what time it is?"

"I'm all ready to eat breakfast," said Dr. Pimplewasser calmly, patting his stomach. "It does feel empty."

"Do you know that it is now 4 o'clock. The eggs have become as hard as rocks and the toast is one lump of charcoal."

"But I'm hungry," said Dr. Pimplewasser.

"I'm sorry," said Mrs. Pimplewasser. "You'll have to wait, for it is now neither time for breakfast, lunch, or supper."

Dr. Pimplewasser saw that he could do nothing with his wife, who was in a determined mood.

He did not have anything to eat until supper. He did not like being hungry.

Before going to bed that night, he made up his mind to get up early enough to eat his breakfast. He had talked over his troubles during the day with a friend, another professor at the university.

"Write everything down on paper. Write down where you put your shoes, your hat, your tie, your shirt," said the professor. "Write everything down. When you get up in the morning, you'll know right away where everything is."

"That is a wonderful idea," said Dr. Pimple-

Z.BLUM.

wasser, delighted. "I'll do exactly what you tell me."

Before going to bed, Dr. Pimplewasser took a long sheet and wrote: "My hat is on the bedroom sofa. My jacket is in the closet. My shoes are near the bed. My socks are in the shoes. My tie is hanging from the back of the easy chair in the bedroom . . ."

Thus did he write everything down. At the end, he wrote very carefully, "I'm in bed."

And then he went to sleep.

When he awoke the next morning, he stretched out his legs, drew a deep breath. As he rubbed his face in his hands, he stopped suddenly. He felt the slip of paper in his hand. He rejoiced. He remembered what the paper contained.

He jumped out of bed and without any trouble, he found everything where it was supposed to be.

"This is wonderful. I'll eat breakfast today," he thought, as he put on his trousers, his shoes, his shirt, his tie, etc. At last, he came to the end of the list. It said, "I'm in bed."

He looked in the bed and he became white. The bed was empty. Dr. Pimplewasser was not there.

"What is the use," he thought, "of knowing where all my clothes are and even having breakfast when I'm lost?"

"Where am I?" he asked, in desperation. "Where am I?"

Finally, he thought, "Maybe I fell under the bed."

He got down on all fours and began to look. Sure enough, there he was—right under the bed.

"Thank heavens!" he cried out, "at last I've found myself."

When he came downstairs all dressed, his wife was fixing the breakfast.

"My, my, you are early," she said. "This is most unusual. I am very happy you managed so well. You'll soon have a piping hot breakfast ready."

Dr. Pimplewasser smiled but said nothing, although anyone could see he was very pleased with himself. "There is no sense worrying my wife," he thought to himself, "by telling her how narrowly I escaped being lost."

"I Won't Have It"

MR. TEMPERLESS WAS ALWAYS SMILING and friendly, while his wife was always scolding and quarreling. He was as kindly and charitable as he was rich. He was always ready to help anyone. His wife, however, was stingy and had a nasty temper. For that reason, Chelm called her Mrs. Hightemper.

Because he was so charitable, his wife was constantly finding fault with him. She had just discovered that he had raised the wages of the servants, which made her furious. While she was scolding him, she heard a knock on the front door. Opening it, she saw a delegation of citizens of Chelm.

"We would like to see Mr. Temperless," they said. To be pleasant, they added: "Nice weather, isn't it?"

"It is the worst weather we have had in the last fifty years," said Mrs. Hightemper, coldly.

She never liked to have anyone call on Mr. Temperless, because she was afraid the visitor might ask him for money. Somewhat reluctantly, she invited them in. If she had known why they had come, she probably would have told them to stay out.

"Good evening, Mr. Temperless," said the members of the delegation, when they were in the house.

"Good evening, my good friends," said Mr. Temperless. "Is there anything I can do for you?"

"We are planning to build, as you know, a hospital," said the citizens of Chelm. "We are asking everyone to contribute as much as he is able. Would you care to donate anything?"

"I shall build the hospital with my own money," said Mr. Temperless. "You are poor and need the money badly. I can well afford to build the hospital myself."

He took the list on which were the names of all the people who had promised to give money and tore it up.

"Your offer is most generous," said the citizens. "You are indeed a noble man!" as they left, they thanked him again and again.

Mrs. Hightemper saw what took place. You can imagine her fury. She was red in the face and bursting with rage.

"It is just like you to give your money away for everything and anything," she cried. "When they want money, they come to you, and you are fool enough to give it. The town, however, never thinks of selecting you for any honor."

"Perhaps they know I have no education and that I am really not very smart," said Mr. Temperless.

"That's just it," flared up his wife. "They like you only for your money. They have no use for you otherwise. You must put a stop to it."

"What shall I do?" asked Mr. Temperless, bewildered.

Mrs. Hightemper thought for a while. "I know," she said, finally. "The next time the town has a meeting you get up and say, 'I won't have it!' No matter what is said or who says it, you bang your fist and say, 'I won't have it! I won't have it!' The town will then see that they have to reckon with you."

"You know," he said, "I never attend meetings. I am altogether too uneducated to help in deciding matters."

"You shall attend the next meeting. I shall see to that," insisted his wife. "And you do exactly as I tell you."

Compelled by his wife, Mr. Temperless came to the next town meeting of Chelm. He sat up front. The people were surprised to see him. They were, however, glad that he had come. Many came up to him, shook his hand and welcomed him. Everyone liked Mr. Temperless.

"It was noble of Mr. Temperless to offer to pay the entire expense of building the hospital," said one citizen, after the meeting was opened. "However, I do not believe that we should allow him to do this. It is not fair. The town should build the hospital."

"That is right," said the others. "The town should build the hospital."

At this point, Mr. Temperless arose, banged his fist, and shouted: "I won't have it! I won't have it!"

Nobody ever saw Mr. Temperless so excited. He shouted so loudly that they gave him permission to build the hospital at his own expense. His generosity made everyone like him even more.

"It is for good reasons that we love Mr. Temperless," said the Mayor, clearing his voice. "I shall regard it as an honor if he consents to come up to the platform and sit with the other distinguished citizens."

"I won't have it! I won't have it!" shouted Mr. Temperless.

This pleased the people still more. He was certainly a modest man! He didn't want anything for himself!

"It seems to me," said one of the citizens, "that Mr. Temperless ought to be our next mayor. I do not believe that there is another person in all Chelm who more richly deserves such an honor. He is kind, generous, and charitable."

The acting mayor, who was chairman of the meeting, was not the least bit insulted. "It is quite true," the Mayor said, "that Mr. Temperless is most fit for this high position."

Mr. Temperless was about to be selected mayor when he arose and began to shout: "I won't have it! I won't have it!"

"You see," said the people, still more pleased with

him, "he does all the kind deeds from the goodness of his heart and doesn't want to be honored for them."

"We are sorry that you don't want to be our mayor," said the chairman. "Perhaps, after thinking it over, you will change your mind. We hope you will. At our next meeting we shall again offer you the position."

When Mr. Temperless arrived home, his wife was waiting for him.

"Well, did you do as I told you?" demanded his wife.

"Yes," said Mr. Temperless. "I did exactly as you told me."

"Now the town shall respect you," said his wife. "You shall soon see that they will select you as mayor."

So certain of this was Mrs. Hightemper that she went with her husband to the next meeting, though the women of Chelm seldom came. She thought it would look nice for her to be present when he became Chelm's mayor. She held her head high and her nose up in the air, as befitted the wife of a high official.

"We are still hoping," said the chairman, "that Mr. Temperless will be our mayor. At the last meeting he refused. We hope that he has changed his mind."

Before the chairman could finish his speech, Mr. Temperless began to shout more loudly and lustily than ever: "I won't have it! I won't have it! I won't have it!"

Mrs. Hightemper tried to hush him up. She grabbed him by the jacket and pulled him back to

his seat. Mr. Temperless, however, was strong and could not be moved. In fact, his wife's pulling made him shout louder than ever. He thought she was pulling his jacket because he wasn't shouting loudly enough.

"Mr. Temperless seems so set on refusing the position," said the chairman, finally, "that we shall have to choose someone else."

After the meeting, Mr. Temperless turned to his wife, and said: "You saw for yourself that I did exactly as you told me."

He expected to be praised. He couldn't understand why his wife was more angry than ever.

Snow Falls in Chelm

THE CHILDREN OF CHELM loved snow very much. But they rarely ever saw snow. Even when there was a big snowstorm, only a few flakes fell, scarcely enough to cover the sidewalk.

During one winter, while the children were at school, snow started falling. Every child hoped that the downfall would not stop. And it didn't. The flakes fell thick and fast, hour after hour. The children were very happy. Even the teachers were happy.

In honor of the occasion, all school work stopped while the children gathered around the windows and watched. Everyone was delighted with the white trees, the white rooftops, the white houses, and the white streets.

"How beautiful the snow is," they said.

The three o'clock bell rang. It was time to go home.

The children marched to the wardrobe, gathered their wraps, buttoned themselves up warmly, and started to leave.

As one of the children marched out into the street, the other children noticed that with every step he made a dent and a mark in the soft snow, which spoiled its smooth appearance. The children didn't like that. Neither did the teachers.

"Come right back! Quick! Quick!" cried the children to their classmate.

"Come right back," commanded the teachers, who loved the snow as much as the children.

Slowly the child came back, taking great care to return by stepping in the little holes he had already made so as not to make any more marks in the fresh, clean snow.

Instead of going home, the children remained in the building. None of them wanted to spoil the snow.

Several hours later worried parents telephoned the school.

"Herbert hasn't come home and I do not know what could have happened," said a mother over the telephone. "I am frantic with worry."

"Has Stanley been kept in school again?" asked another mother. "If he has, it will be better for him to stay there. I intend to give him the thrashing of his life, which ought to teach him never to be naughty again."

The principal explained matters.

Since the parents loved snow as much as the

children and the teachers, they all said: "See that the children do not spoil the snow."

As hours passed, not only did the parents become anxious, but the children became hungry. The sun had set and it was fast becoming dark and still the children were in school. How long could they remain here, especially when they were becoming more and more hungry?

Finally, one of the bright children said: "I have an idea."

The lad was the brightest child in the school. Everyone said that when he grew up he would probably be selected as one of the Wise Men.

"Good," said the teachers, encouragingly.

"Good," said the hungry children.

"What is it?" asked the children.

"What is it?" asked the teachers.

"We are practically prisoners here in school," said the bright child, "because we do not want to spoil the snow."

"Even the most stupid child knows that," said the teachers, disappointed.

"Yes, I know that, too," said the dunce, proudly.

"That doesn't help us," said the teachers and the children.

"Why can't we hire men to carry us on their shoulders?" asked the bright child.

"What will happen when we do that?" asked the teachers and the children.

"Let me explain," said the bright child. "None of us is going home because we do not want to spoil the snow. If each one of us were carried on the shoulders of someone else, none of our feet

would reach the snow and the snow would not be spoiled. We should hire men to carry us home."

"That's an excellent idea," agreed the teachers and the children.

The principal hired the men. The children climbed on the men's shoulders and thus they were carried home.

In this way, the children of Chelm avoided spoiling the snow.

As for the bright child who thought of the idea, his teacher gave him an A for school work and awarded him five gold stars, which was more than she had given to any child since she had been teaching. But no other child had ever thought of such a good idea!

Chelm's School

ONE MORNING Mr. Temperless came home very excited and unhappy. He had returned from a trip to several neighboring towns.

"Good wife," he said, "they are spreading falsehoods about us."

"What do you mean 'about us'? I keep my home clean. You pay your bills. You are charitable and kind . . ."

"You do not understand. They do not speak of you and me but about our town."

"What are they saying?"

"I get angry when I think of it. They are saying that the people who live here are stupid. Can you imagine! We, the people of Chelm are stupid!"

"We do things differently from every other town. We do nothing as other towns do. That shows we are smart," said his wife. "In all other towns horses and wagons are driven on the wide road, but in our town we drive them on the sidewalk. In all other towns . . ."

She wanted to go on, but her husband interrupted her.

"That is one of the things they say is foolish about our town."

"Didn't you explain to them why we have arranged it so?"

"I did, but they still didn't understand."

"That shows how foolish they are. The road is big and wide; the sidewalk is narrow. Who is more important—a human being or a horse? For that reason we have the people walk on the wide, broad road. Let the horses and wagons use the narrow sidewalk. Now, isn't that smart?"

"That should be plain to anyone, but they didn't agree with me."

They both went out and told everybody they met what Mr. Temperless had found out.

You can imagine how angry and indignant that made the people.

"These lies must stop," they cried.

"We shall show them," said the Wise Men of Chelm. "We shall build a school. And what a school! The biggest and the best in the whole country! One look at that school should convince everyone that we are the wisest men and women who have ever lived."

The next thing they had to do was to decide on where to build the school.

The Wise Men thought and thought and they finally figured out that the best place for a school would be the center of the town.

"If the school were built in the center," explained the Wise Men, "one child would not have to walk a long distance and another one a short distance. It would be the same for everyone. That would make it most fair."

Workmen soon began digging the foundation for the new school, which would stand as a monument to the wisdom of Chelm. Soon an excited citizen, named Mr. Bigwig, rushed up, held up his hands and shouted: "Stop! Stop!"

At first the workmen thought an accident had happened, and they scattered in all directions. After they had run for some distance, they realized that they didn't know why or where they were going. Hence, they began to return to the spot from where they had started to run.

When they had reassembled, they started digging again. Once more Mr. Bigwig raised his hands in the air wildly and shouted: "Stop! Stop!"

The workmen, however, were not fooled twice. This time they asked Mr. Bigwig what was the matter.

"Did not our Wise Men decide to build the school in the center of the town?" he exclaimed.

"That is so," answered the workmen.

"This isn't the center," roared Mr. Bigwig.

"We figured out, Mr. Bigwig, that it was," replied the workmen, politely.

"Never!" roared Mr. Bigwig, louder than ever.

"Where is the center?" asked the workmen.

"My house!" exclaimed Mr. Bigwig. "Listen carefully," he continued, "and you shall see clearly that I am right. If anyone wants to come to my house, he must come to my house and no other house. If he goes to any other house, he wouldn't be in my house. Say you lived on the north side of the town, another person on the south side, a third person on the west, and a fourth on the east. All of you—from north, south, east, and west—would have to meet at my house. So my house, as you see, is the center of the town."

"That is right," agreed the workmen.

The workmen began digging the foundation for the new school near Mr. Bigwig's house. They hadn't been digging long when another man came rushing up to them, shouting wildly: "Don't dig another shovelful. You have made a mistake. This isn't the center at all."

"Where is the center?" asked the workmen.

"My house!" exclaimed the man. "I am surprised that you are so foolish as not to have perceived it immediately."

The workmen looked around dumbfounded, not knowing what to say.

"If a person wants to come to my house," explained the man, "he must come to my house, no matter where he lives. If he lived in China and wanted to come to my house, he would have to cross the Pacific Ocean, come to Chelm, find my house and walk into it. My house may be a humble place. Yet this man, even if he entered the magnicent mansion of our mayor, would be in the mayor's house, but not in mine. No matter where a person lived—Africa, Europe, the North Pole, or Australia —he would have to come to my house, that is, if he wanted to come to my house. For that reason as you see, my house is the center, not only of this town, but of the world."

The workmen listened patiently. "Ah! Ah!" they cried. "We perceive now. The man talks wisely. His house is truly the center."

After digging for a short while near the man's house, the workers were interrupted by many other people who shouted, "My house is the center." "No, my house is the center."

By this time the workers were bewildered and disgusted. The problem was becoming too much for them. Needing advice, they went, as everyone else did, to the Wise Men of Chelm.

The Wise Men thought and thought. After long deliberation, they decided it wasn't a simple matter to decide on the spot which was the center of the town.

"Since we, the Wise Men, ruled that a school should be built, a school must be built," they declared. "Since we also ruled that the school should be built in the center of the town, it must be built in the center of the town. However, we can't waste time now deciding what spot is the center. Therefore, we have agreed, in order not to delay the workmen, to build the school outside of the town. By the time the school is finished, we shall have decided where the center of the town is. Then, we shall move the school from outside of the town to the center of the town. In this way we shall not waste a minute's time."

The town marveled at the wisdom of their Wise Men.

The following morning the workmen began building the school outside of the city. Now no one disturbed them.

By the time the school was finished everyone

had agreed that the center of the town was a mountain which was on the Main Street. On a set day, all the good people were ordered to gather at the school with wagons, shovels, scooping machinery, and such things.

When the people saw the school, they liked it almost as much as they did their town hall. Everything about the building was new and shiny. The paint was fresh and had hardly dried.

The people were about to push the building from its foundation, when one of the Wise Men said: "As I think of it, we may scratch the woodwork and soil the newly-painted walls by moving the school."

"That is so," said the people, who hated the idea of disturbing this beautiful new building. "What shall we do?" they asked.

Then and there, one of the Wise Men stroked his beard and exclaimed, "I have it."

"Have what?" asked the others.

"An idea! Instead of moving the school to the center of the town, let us move the center of the town to the school."

"An excellent idea," said everyone.

All the people, carrying their axes, shovels, and picks, went to the mountain, which, as you remember, was the center of the town. Hour after hour they dug, scooped and moved the rock. Soon they began to perspire and they removed their coats and jackets.

Two tramps, who were passing, saw the clothing and walked away with it.

The people of Chelm continued to shovel the center of the town to the school. Sometime later, one of the men looked up and could not see his coat and jacket, nor could he see anyone else's coat and jacket.

"My!" he exclaimed. "What a great distance we have moved this mountain! We have moved it so far that we can't even see our clothing."

Another person looked around and said: "We certainly have moved the center of the town far enough."

"Yes," the others agreed. "It is time to stop."

And this they all gladly did.

That's how the people of Chelm built their school in the center of the town without really building it in the center of the town.

Chelm's Farmer
Awaits a Relative

SHARPY WEISELHEAD, a farmer in Chelm, was surprised when the mailman stopped in front of his house.

"No," he called out, "I haven't any letters. Who has told you that I want to write you one?"

Chelm's mailman smiled, as if something was happening which very seldom happened. "I have a letter for you, and I would like one in return," he said, becoming serious.

In Chelm, when the mailman gave you a letter, you had to give him one. That's how the mailman always did business.

Mr. Weiselhead, however, could not write.

"I'll give you a basket of fruit for the letter," he said.

The mailman agreed and the bargain was made. When the mailman left, Mr. Weiselhead excitedly called to his wife: "Tippy Pappippy! Tippy Pappippy! See how important I am! The mailman has brought me a letter. Help me read it."

Tippy Pappippy instantly dropped everything she was doing and ran to her husband. Both were so excited they trembled. Mrs. Tippy Pappippy did not open the envelope and take out the letter. She tore the whole thing into many parts, and then carefully took out each piece from the envelope. Then she pasted the pieces together.

"It would take too long to open the envelope," she explained. "It is better and easier to tear the whole thing up and paste it together again."

She now began to read the pasted letter.

"I am becoming very old," said the letter. "Before I die I should like to see you and your wife. I shall therefore visit you for several days. I shall then know to whom I ought to leave my money and property when I die. My train will arrive at three o'clock Friday afternoon. Please meet me at the station."

The letter ended like this: "Your good friend, Cuppy Weiselhead."

"Where did I hear of Weiselhead before?" said Mr. Weiselhead, thinking hard. "The name sounds very familiar."

Mr. Sharpy Weiselhead began to throw one chair across the room, and then another and then another. When he had finished throwing the chairs around, he began upsetting the dining room table. Whenever Mr. Weiselhead thought, he always threw furniture topsy-turvy. He said it helped him to think. But still he couldn't remember who Cuppy Weiselhead was. This made him so angry that he grabbed an axe and was about to smash the walls of his house.

Just then he remembered.

"Now I know who Cuppy Weiselhead is," he cried, dropping the axe. "It is lucky that I do remember. If I didn't, I would have had to ruin the whole house. Cuppy Weiselhead is my uncle, whom I love very much and whom I know as well as I know you, my wife."

You can imagine how hard Mr. Sharpy Weiselhead would have had to think and how much furniture he would have had to break if he hadn't known and hadn't loved his uncle so well.

"By all means I shall meet him at the station," he said to his wife.

As soon as he found some time to spare, he hitched the wagon to his horse and began riding to the railroad station.

Proudly, he told everyone he met that he had received a letter that morning.

"I am now going to meet my uncle," he explained.

Not everyone, you should understand, received letters in Chelm, nor did everyone have an uncle for whom to wait. Because of this everyone congratulated him.

As he approached the station, he became more and more excited. He stopped people whom he did not even know.

One of them was a stranger passing through Chelm.

"When is your uncle arriving?" asked the stranger.

"Don't you know?" asked Farmer Sharpy Weiselhead, astonished. "It says right here in the letter—

Friday. You can't live in Chelm, for people here are altogether too smart to ask such a stupid question."

"What day is today?" continued the stranger.

Mr. Sharpy Weiselhead looked down on the man, as if he were a dunce. "Even a child knows that this is Thursday."

"If your uncle is coming Friday," said the man, puzzled, "why are you meeting him on Thursday?"

Mr. Sharply Weiselhead was more disgusted than ever. He was sorry that he had told this stranger anything. "I have no time to meet my uncle on Friday," he said somewhat angrily. "Why can't you understand so simple a matter? But today, Thursday, I have some spare hours. So instead of Friday, I am going to meet my uncle today."

Mr. Sharply Weiselhead, glad to be rid of the stranger, kept on riding to the railroad station, shaking his head and wondering how stupid those people could be who lived outside of Chelm.

Mr. Spindlethread's Wooden Bed

Mr. Spindlethread, the carpenter of Chelm, sleeps on a wooden bed. He does not allow a mattress, a pillow, or anything soft near him. His bed is one piece of hard wood and the harder the wood the better he likes it. This is the reason:

One time Mr. Spindlethread was lost in a strange town. He went from house to house to find shelter, but everyone turned him away. He kept on wandering until night. He was tired and weary. He came to a forest, but he did not want to enter because he might get lost. He was so weary that he was ready to fall to the ground and make the ground his bed. Just then he saw a bench. He crawled to the bench and stretched himself out full length and was soon fast asleep.

When he awoke at dawn, every part of his body was sore and ached.

"I never feel like this when I get up in my own bed in the morning," he said to himself.

He examined the bench carefully in order to find out what made him so tired. He looked and looked but found nothing. After much searching, he discovered a little feather. He held up the feather and carefully inspected it.

"Ah," he said, "now I understand why I am not rested. It's this feather that has disturbed me."

When he reached home, he gave away his own bed, with its soft downy cover, its feathery pillow, its fine feathery mattress. He built a hard wooden bench, and refused to sleep on anything but that.

"If one feather," he explained, "makes me so tired, just imagine what a whole bedful of feathers can do."

A Blacksmith Moves
into Chelm

A BLACKSMITH MOVED into Chelm.

When the people heard about this, they became very frightened.

"Everyone knows that the blacksmith is a thief," they said. "None of us is safe."

Of course, no one knows anything of the kind. To you and to me and to every sensible person, a blacksmith is like everyone else. But by now you should know that the people of Chelm are not like everyone else, and they do not think as everyone else does.

"We must watch our belongings so that that blacksmith does not steal from us," they said. They did not go to sleep; they remained awake all night watching. In the morning, they were so sleepy that they could barely stand up. While at work, many fell asleep. Some dozed in the middle of the street. The street-cleaner was found with his head in a refuse can snoring loudly. While dropping some litter into the can, he had become so drowsy that he dropped off into sleep before he could pick his head up.

Their eyes drooping, scarcely able to stand up, the people of Chelm gathered before their Wise Men.

"We can't stand this any longer," they said. "You must do something for us."

"Why can't you sleep?" asked the Wise Men of Chelm.

"Don't you know why?" they answered, obviously astonished. "Even we plain, ordinary people know why. That blacksmith is a thief and we must watch him day and night.

The Wise Men of Chelm stroked their long white beards and they thought and thought.

At last one of them said: "I have an idea that shall remedy matters. It takes a wise man to think of what I have thought."

At this point, he patted himself on the back because nobody else did.

"It is quite true that the workers must work by day," he said, "And it is quite true that at night they must watch the blacksmith. Since the store-keepers are their own bosses, they can work any time they wish. They don't have to keep their stores open by day; they can keep their stores open at night. After the workers have come home and have eaten their supper and are ready to go to bed, the storekeepers can then open their stores. While they have their stores open, they can watch the blacksmith so that he does not steal. In this way, the workers can get their regular sleep during the night and the storekeepers can get their sleep during the day. Everyone—the storekeepers and the workers—will have a time for sleep. And the blacksmith will be watched day and night and all of you will feel safe."

The Wise Men of Chelm were very proud of themselves that they could think of such a clever idea.

And the people of Chelm went away delighted.

All went well for awhile but soon there was trouble.

The storekeepers came in one great mass to the Wise Men and shouted: "That blacksmith! That blacksmith!"

"What now?" asked the Wise Men. "Did not we mend matters?"

"Not at all," they exclaimed. "You have ruined us. During the night, when we have our store open, all the workmen are asleep and nobody buys from us. Our stores are empty. We cannot pay rent. We cannot buy food for our children. You must do something for us."

After much thinking, one of the Wise Men slowly rose from his chair, stroked his long beard, and said: "I have an idea. The storekeepers want to keep their stores open by day."

"Everybody knows that," said the other Wise Men, disappointed. "Don't forget that you are now talking to the smartest men in Chelm and you mustn't say silly things."

"I know that," said the man with the idea. "I shall give you only my best and finest ideas. Let me proceed. If the workmen worked at night instead of by day, the storekeepers will then be able to keep their stores open by day as they want to. In this way, the storekeepers will be able to watch the blacksmith by day while they keep their stores open, and by night, while they are at work, the workers will be able to watch. So the blacksmith will be watched day and night and everyone will feel safe and no one will lose any sleep."

The storekeepers went away happy and content.

Several days later, the storekeepers again came to the Wise Men of Chelm, more angry than ever.

"What's the trouble now?" asked the Wise Men. "We thought we had settled matters."

"We are ruined," they cried. "We cannot pay rent. Our children have no food. When we keep our stores open by day, the workmen are asleep, and they do not buy from us. Our stores are empty."

The Wise Men of Chelm saw that they were confronted by a very difficult problem. They carefully oiled their thinking machinery so that it would work perfectly. Sure enough, they soon hit upon the smartest idea that had ever occurred to them.

"Why can't we hire a watchman to watch the blacksmith?" they said. "If we did that, the workers will be able to work by day and sleep by night; and the storekeepers will be able to keep their stores open by day as they used to."

And this was what was done.

The town hired a watchman. He was a very old man who could hardly walk.

At last all of Chelm was again at peace and all were content. The workmen were happy that they could again sleep at night, and the storekeepers were happy that they could again do business.

And Chelm was prouder of their Wise Men than ever.

Soon, however, there was trouble.

The Watchman came to the Wise Men and said that he didn't want to watch anymore. "I don't want the job."

"Why?" asked the Wise Men, dumbfounded. "Are you wages too low?"

"No," said the Watchman. "That's not it at all. I should like to ask you a question."

"By all means," said the Wise Men.

"When am I supposed to watch the blacksmith?"

"At night, of course," said one of the Wise Men, insulted that he should be asked such a simple question.

"But it is sometimes cold at night," said the Watchman. "While I am out at night watching the blacksmith, I may catch cold and the cold may turn into pneumonia and I may die. No, I don't want the job."

Saying this, he walked out of the room and went home.

Again the people of Chelm could not sleep.

The Wise Men thought harder than ever, and after many days of thinking, one of them exclaimed:

"I have it!"

"What have you?" asked the others, puzzled.

"An idea. Why doesn't the Watchman want to watch?"

"Because he's liable to catch cold and the cold

may turn into pneumonia and he may die," said the others.

"We'll buy him a sheepskin overcoat and that will keep him warm on cold nights and he won't catch cold and he won't die from pneumonia."

And so it was done.

The Watchman, now satisfied, began to watch the blacksmith.

But soon there was trouble.

The Watchman again refused to watch.

"What's the matter now?" the Wise Men asked.

"It's that sheepskin coat," he replied.

"But we bought that for you," said the Wise Men, "so that you wouldn't catch cold, so that you wouldn't catch pneumonia and die."

"That may be true," said the Watchman, "but did you notice what kind of a coat the blacksmith wears?"

"A sheepskin coat," said the Wise Men, remembering.

"Exactly," said the Watchman, with a shrug of his shoulders. "I'm not as wise as you are, but I am not as foolish as you think I am. Everybody knows that the blacksmith is a thief. If the blacksmith were caught stealing, they might shoot at me instead of at him. The sheepskin coat, as you see, might prove the undoing of me."

The workers now had to remain awake all night. Nobody knew what to do.

The Wise Men, however, thought of a remedy. "Let the Watchman wear his sheepskin coat inside out, with the sheepskin on the outside. When he wears it this way, not even a fool will be able to mistake our Watchman for the blacksmith."

And so it was done.

The Watchman returned to his job and all was well.

Soon again the Watchman wanted to quit. "You know," he said to the Wise Men, "I wear my sheepskin coat inside out. Foxes prowl around at night. Everyone knows that foxes eat sheep. They might mistake me for a sheep and eat me. No, I don't want to watch."

Chelm was again in despair and again the Wise Men began to think.

"We'll buy the Watchman a horse," they said, "and we'll put him on the horse wearing his sheepskin coat inside out. Even foxes know that sheep don't ride on horses, so they'll let him alone."

And so it was done and all was well.

But soon the Watchman again refused to watch.

"What is the matter now?" asked the Wise Men, somewhat angrily.

"I ride on a horse, don't I?" he asked.

"Yes, so that foxes may not mistake you for a sheep."

"While riding on the horse," said the Watchman, "I may become sleepy and fall off. A person can die from falling off a horse as well as from pneumonia."

This time one of the Wise Men had an idea right away. "I know how to avoid the danger. Let us tie the Watchman to the horse with a strong rope. Then, he don't be able to fall, even if he wanted."

Again all was well. The Wise Men particularly rejoiced. Now they could take a rest from thinking. They never had had to think as much as they did

lately. But the quiet and the peace did not last for long.

The Watchman appeared another time before the Wise Men. "We are glad to see you," they said. A moment later they were sorry they had made the remark, for the Watchman was angrier than ever, and nobody is ever glad to see an angry person.

"You want to kill me!" he cried. "You put me on a horse and then you tie me to the horse. You know as well as I that at night lions and tigers prowl in the forests. If the horse should wander into the forest, the lions and tigers might attack me, and I won't even be able to jump down from the horse and run away."

Seeing that the Watchman was very angry, the Wise Men immediately thought of an idea. "We'll tie you," they said, "to the horse, and the horse we'll tie to the post on Main Street."

"The lions and tigers won't be able to eat me, will they?" asked the Watchman, trembling.

The Wise Men laughed at the silly question. "How could the horse ever reach the forest when it is tied to a post?"

This made the Watchman feel much better. Now he was happy to be Chelm's Watchman. Night after night, the Watchman—tied to his horse, the horse tied to a post—stood guard.

One morning great crowds, dressed in night-clothes, came rushing to the street shouting, "Where is the Watchman? Where is the Watchman?"

They found him on Main Street, tied to his horse, the horse tied to a post.

"We have been robbed," they cried, shaking their fists at him.

"All my clothes have been taken from my house," said one man, wearing pajamas.

"All my silverware has been stolen," cried another.

"Why are we paying you?" demanded a third.

"You are supposed to watch the blacksmith and instead you are here," said still another.

They decided to take the Watchman to the judge, who would know what punishment to mete out to him.

"Where were you when the robbery took place?" asked the judge, sternly.

"On the horse, which was tied to the post," answered the Watchman.

"Why were you tied to the post?"

"So that the horse shouldn't wander into the forests, where lions and tigers might have attacked me."

"Why were you tied to the horse?"

"So I shouldn't fall off."

"Why were you on the horse in the first place?"

"Because I didn't want the foxes to eat me."

"Why should the foxes eat you?"

"Because I wore a sheepskin coat inside out and the foxes might mistake me for a sheep."

"Why did you wear the sheepskin coat inside out?"

"Because I didn't want anyone to mistake me for the blacksmith, who also wore a sheepskin coat."

"Why did you wear a sheepskin coat?"

"Because I didn't want to catch cold and die from pneumonia."

The judge saw that he had a reason for everything he did.

"It is not all towns," said the judge proudly, "who can have so smart a watchman. I hereby order that his salary be raised."

The people saw that the judge was right, and at the next election chose the Watchman as the mayor of Chelm because he was so smart.

Chelm Tries to Arrest
a Thief

THE PEOPLE OF CHELM hadn't forgotten the black-smith who had robbed them. A man who steals, they said, is a thief, and if he is a thief—why, he is a thief. They stopped because they couldn't think of anything else to say. If the blacksmith had stolen when they hadn't a watchman, they could forgive him. Anyone, however, who stole when they had hired a watchman wasn't fair or honest. For that reason, they were most anxious to punish him. A big reward was offered for the blacksmith's arrest.

Every policeman wanted to win this reward. Not only would he receive a lot of money, but he would be a hero at the same time.

One day Chelm's captain of police saw the blacksmith walking down the street.

"Ah!" he said to himself, "this is my lucky day!"

Holding him securely by the arm, he roared: "Aren't you a blacksmith?"

"No," said the blacksmith.

The captain of police was downcast for a moment. He thought of his wife and children who would not be able to buy the new clothes which he had planned to buy with the reward. In his imagination, he had already spent the money.

"What are you?" he asked.

"I am retired," said the blacksmith.

"What do you mean 'retired'?" asked the captain, puzzled. It was a big word and he did not understand what it meant.

"'Retired' means doing nothing. I do not work. I have made enough money to live without working."

The captain was about to let him go when he thought of asking: "You were, however, once a blacksmith and stole from the people of Chelm?"

"That is true," replied the blacksmith.

"No one can fool me that way," the captain said to himself, his chest swelling with pride. "Come along to the judge," he said to the blacksmith, pulling him by the arm.

While walking, the blacksmith said: "I am hungry. I must have something to eat."

"Can't you wait until you reach the station house?" the captain asked.

"No," said the blacksmith, as he stopped in front of a restaurant. "I can't take another step unless I have something to eat."

"Are you sure you can't wait?" asked the captain.

"I am certain. Please, let me get a bite to eat," pleaded the blacksmith.

"First, you must promise on your word of honor that you will not try to escape," said the captain.

"I promise."

They entered the restaurant. The blacksmith ordered food, and when he was through eating, he said: "I shall now go and pay the cashier. But you, Mr. Captain, needn't come with me. You can rest here awhile longer."

"Are you sure it is all right?" asked the captain, uncertainly.

"Perfectly all right," the blacksmith assured him.

"No monkey business now!" warned the captain in a stern voice, as the blacksmith walked away.

The captain sat at the table and waited and waited—and waited. Three hours passed, four hours passed, five hours passed. It was almost midnight and the restaurant was about to close.

"My wife will surely be worried," the captain thought. "Maybe the blacksmith is lost and cannot find me."

Finally, he got up from the table and searched the whole restaurant, but the blacksmith was nowhere to be seen.

At last, he went up to the cashier.

"Yes," she said, "I remember the man for whom you are looking. He paid his bill many hours ago and went out by the front door."

"The low-down thief!" ejaculated the captain of police, bellowing with rage. "He didn't even keep his word. He is thoroughly dishonest. It serves me right. I shouldn't have any business with dishonest people."

Several days later, the captain again caught the

blacksmith. "You shall not escape this time," he said to him sternly.

In front of a restaurant, the blacksmith stopped walking and said: "I am thirsty and hungry. I cannot take another step unless I have food."

"Are you sure that you can't take even one more step?" asked the captain of police.

"Certainly! I am positive," roared the blacksmith.

"Can I trust you not to escape this time?" asked the captain.

"I promise on my word of honor."

They were about to walk into the restaurant, when the captain of police stopped.

"This time I am going to make sure that you won't escape. I shall wait for you outside the restaurant."

The thief went inside alone.

The captain of police waited and waited and waited. It was evening and dark and it had begun to rain. The captain was cold and hungry.

"That blacksmith must be eating a house. I know it is impolite, but I can't wait any longer. I shall go inside and hurry him along."

In the restaurant, the blacksmith was nowhere to be seen. The cashier did not remember his leaving, neither did the waiters. The cook, who was in the back of the restaurant, did remember him. "The blacksmith," she said, "went out by the back door."

"He must have escaped," said the captain of police, beginning to understand. "That is why he went out through the back door. He knew I was at the front door. It serves me right. I shouldn't have any business with thieves."

Several days later the captain again caught the blacksmith walking down Main Street.

This time he was very angry. "I don't care how hungry you are. You cannot go into any more restaurants," he exclaimed. "You shall have to wait until you arrive at the station house."

They hadn't walked more than a block when the blacksmith was again hungry and refused to walk unless he had something to eat.

"If your child was hungry," pleaded the blacksmith of the chief of police, "what would you think of a person who wouldn't let him eat?"

The captain, although he appeared severe, had at bottom a tender heart. He thought of his two daughters and his son and felt badly.

"How shall I know you won't escape?" he asked.

"I'll give you my word of honor."

"You gave me your word before and you didn't keep it," said the captain.

"This time, however, I mean it."

"Didn't you mean a word of it before?" asked the captain, trying hard to understand.

"My! How smart you are!" said the blacksmith. "That's exactly so."

They were both about to enter the restaurant, when the captain stopped. "No," he said, his brow creased from deep thinking, "this will never do. Despite what you tell me, I can't trust your word of honor. I shall show you how smart we policemen of Chelm are. You won't get away this time. No sir! You stay outside the restaurant and I'll go inside and bring the food out to you. And make sure you wait. I won't be gone for more than a minute."

The captain went inside while the thief remained outside.

Soon the captain returned. He looked all around for the blacksmith.

"Why, he is not here!" the captain exclaimed, almost bursting with rage. Then, he thought: "I'm sure when he gave his word of honor, he didn't mean it, like all the other times."

The captain of police went to the mayor and told him the entire story.

"Of course," said the mayor, who understood everything, "you must have three policemen to capture the blacksmith, one to stay with him in the restaurant, another to wait outside and a third to watch the back door. Don't bother with him when you are alone."

In this way, the blacksmith was able to move about town as freely as the most honest citizen. When people asked the captain why he didn't arrest him, he said: "It's no use trying unless you have three policemen."

"Why?" asked the people.

"One must be with him inside the restaurant, a second must be outside and a third must be in the back of the restaurant."

"Why must he be taken to the restaurant?" they asked.

"Because he is always hungry," explained the captain, irritated at their stupidity.

"Ah!" said the people. "Now we understand."

A Bird Disturbs the Wise Men

In Chelm there was one great big building called a skyscraper. It was especially built for the Wise Men. When they thought of something serious and important, they would do their thinking on a high floor. If it was about a little thing that wasn't important or didn't matter much, they would do their thinking on a low floor. Now they were meeting on the sixtieth floor, which is very high up indeed; in fact, it was the very top floor of the skyscraper.

The Wise Men had remained on the top floor all day, arguing and thinking, arguing and thinking. The whirring and the clattering of their thinking machinery could be heard all over town.

In order not to disturb them, the good people of Chelm were walking on tiptoe and talking in whispers.

Here is what the Wise Men were discussing: "What color shoelaces shall we wear tomorrow?"

As they were deep in thought, one of the younger Wise Men noticed a bird flying around the room. It was unbelievable, for no one would ever dare to disturb the Wise Men while they were thinking.

"There is a bird in the room," said the younger Wise Man. "Has anyone invited him?"

"No," said the other Wise Men, shocked that such a thing could happen.

"What is he doing here?" asked the others, by now aroused. "He has come without an invitation. He is an impolite and an impertinent bird."

With motions of their hands, they signaled the bird to leave immediately. They then settled down to their business, certain that the bird would not remain a minute after being so rudely dismissed.

A little later the younger Wise Man looked up and sure enough, the bird was still in the room. "The bird is still here," he cried out.

"What an ill-mannered bird," exclaimed the Wise Men, as they motioned to him to leave. The bird did not pay the slightest attention. Instead he settled himself on the bald head of one of the wisest of the Wise Men, who tried to catch him. The bird lightly flew away and landed on top of a picture.

"Why, he is mocking us!" cried the Wise Men, red with anger. "This will never do. We shall have to teach that bird a lesson."

The Wise Men stopped what they were doing and they all tried to capture their uninvited and unwelcome guest. But the bird was agile. As soon as someone came near enough to reach him, he flew away. The Wise Men climbed on chairs and one another's backs. The bird calmly flew from one object to another. All this increased the anger of the Wise Men. At last, they caught him.

The question arose: What was to be done with the bird?

You could depend on the Wise Men to find an answer. All they need do was to think. And think they did.

Soon one said: "The other day I saw a flower pot fall from the window to the street and it split into a hundred pieces. This bird is not worthy of pity; not after what he has done to us. We ought to throw the bird out of the window and, like the flower pot, he too will break into a hundred pieces. We shall not be troubled with him anymore."

Holding the bird securely in his hand, the younger Wise Man opened the window, extended his hand through it, and with a determined thrust, threw the bird downward, saying as he did this: "It hurts us to treat you in this fashion, but it serves you right. This should be a lesson to you."

After he had done this, the younger Wise Man brushed his hands, as if to clean himself of dirt, and then he joined the other Wise Men, who had now returned to their task of arguing and thinking, arguing and thinking. They still hadn't decided what color shoelaces to wear tomorrow.

They felt much better, however, since they were sure that they would no longer be disturbed.

A little later one of the bald-headed Wise Men felt something tickle him on the top of his head. He scratched. He felt better. Soon something was again tickling him. He scratched again. When he chanced to look up, sure enough, there was the same bird merrily flying around. It acted as if nothing had happened. Certainly, it showed no signs of even being hurt.

The Wise Men were now more angry than ever. They tried to catch the bird with a ladder. In doing so, one of the Wise Men fell, hurting himself painfully. The bird flew on top of a bookcase. When they tried to reach him, the bookcases tumbled down, scattering books all over the room. At last the bird was caught. By now the room was a wreck, and several of the Wise Men were holding their hands to their bruised sides, knees, heads.

"The bird probably stayed on the ledge and didn't fall off at all," explained the younger Wise Man, who had caught the bird and was holding it in his hand. "He shall not fool us this time."

He took the bird and threw it out of the window, making sure that it was thrown over the ledge.

A few minutes later the bird returned.

The Wise Men were furious. "The bird is laughing at us," they moaned. "Doesn't he know that we are the Wise Men of Chelm? Why isn't he dead? When the flower pot fell from a much smaller building, it broke into a hundred pieces? Why isn't the bird split into a hundred pieces?"

"I am beginning to understand," said the youngest Wise Man, as he stroked his beardless face. "The flower pot fell all the way to the ground. I believe that this bird is playing a trick on us. He doesn't fall to the bottom. He stops falling half way down and doesn't even touch the ground. How can you expect him to be crushed when he does that?"

"We understand. We understand," said the other Wise Men, brimming over with delight. "The bird is fooling us, the Wise Men of Chelm. The impertinence! The impudence!"

"Do not worry," said the youngest Wise Man. "The bird shall not get away this time."

After catching the bird, he went to the window, opened it wide, climbed to the ledge, and said: "This bird has fooled us long enough. It shall be his last trick. I shall myself jump down with him and I shall see that he falls all the way. He shall then be crushed into a hundred pieces, as he deserves to be."

Holding the bird securely in his hand so as to make sure that he would not get away, the youngest Wise Man jumped from the window of the sixtieth story.

The other Wise Men settled down to discuss what color shoelaces they ought to wear tomorrow. They were now absolutely sure that the bird would not return. Among other things, they expressed their delight with the wisdom shown by the youngest of the Wise Men. "In a few years," they said, "he will be as wise as we are."

Carrying Bricks

A STRANGER VISITING Chelm saw a man take a handful of bricks from a large pile near a barn and carry them for about a hundred feet to another pile.

"Why are you carrying these bricks?" the stranger asked.

"My, my," said the man, "I always knew that the people outside of Chelm ask foolish questions but I never knew that anyone could ask so foolish a question! Don't you know I am building a house right here at the spot where I am gathering the bricks? For thirty days I have been carrying the bricks from the barn and now you ask me why. To build a brick house everyone knows you must have bricks."

"That was what I thought you were doing," said the stranger.

"Then why did you ask me?" said the man, by now disgusted and ready to walk away with another handful of bricks. "You are keeping me from my work."

"I asked because I noticed a wheelbarrow nearby. Is it yours?"

"Of course it's mine. It has been mine ever since it was new. I bought it."

"If that is so," said the stranger, "you can carry the bricks from one pile to another with the help of the wheelbarrow. In this way, you will be able to carry more bricks and you will find it much easier."

The man's face lighted up.

"I never thought of that. It's a fine idea." He thanked the stranger profusely. "I shall do exactly as you tell me."

When the stranger went away, he started to carry the pile of bricks by hand from the spot where he planned to build his house to the barn, from where, as you remember, he had originally taken them. He carried one handful of bricks; and then another handful of bricks; and then another handful of bricks; and then another handful of bricks and then another, and another, and another. Day after day, he carried and carried and carried, until all the bricks were back again in a neat pile near the barn.

"I shall now start out afresh," he said with satisfaction. "How silly it is to carry a few bricks at a time by hand. I'll now take my wheelbarrow, fill it high up with bricks, and I shall be able to carry many at a time. It should not take me nearly as long to take all the bricks from the barn and bring them to the spot where I'm going to build my house."

As he happily wheeled his load of bricks, he kept on marveling: "How much easier and quicker it is! I cannot understand why a smart man like me did not think of the idea first."

The Man Who Went
to Heaven

ONE DAY AN OLD, feeble horse fell down, and in falling, turned over, standing on its head for a little while. Several people saw this and were amazed.

"Never," said they, "have we seen a horse do tricks, and such tricks!"

Hadn't they seen with their own eyes a horse stand on its head! What couldn't they do—what money couldn't they make—with such a horse! From town to town they would go, giving performances, and they all would be rich. Oh! if they only owned that horse!

They went over to the stranger and said: "We know this is an unusual horse and you would not want to part from it but we are prepared to offer you quite a sum of money for it."

The stranger, as you can imagine, was glad to

sell his horse, as it was sickly and it had not long to live.

"Not every horse," explained the people, "can stand on its head."

Such talk puzzled the stranger, but he remembered the way in which his horse had fallen. "I am dealing with the people of Chelm," he thought to himself, "and they are ready to believe anything."

He became very stubborn and demanded a great sum of money for his horse. "Yes," he insisted, "a horse that can stand on its head is worth a lot of money."

"Yes, yes, that is right," they said. They were glad to pay him what he wanted.

Very happy with their bargain, they led the horse to the center of the town.

The animal fell several times but never on its head.

"That poor old horse!" one child exclaimed. "It is so feeble that it cannot stand on its legs."

"Such foolishness," shouted the townspeople. "Children should not discuss things they cannot understand."

But when the horse lay down and remained lying they all became certain that the child was right.

This made them very angry with the stranger, and they went out in a great crowd to capture him. "We'll do something to him," they cried.

When at last they spied the stranger, they saw him whispering something to a rabbit who raced away. And then almost immediately, as if it came out of his elbow, appeared another rabbit.

The people were fascinated. They asked: "What has happened?"

"You will not understand," said the stranger.

"Oh, yes, we will," they pleaded. "We are not as stupid as some think."

"If that is true, I'll tell you. You saw that rabbit. It is trained. It has just run an errand for me, and it has come back, as you see, with an answer."

"What? That is wonderful," said the people of Chelm. "It is even better than a horse that does tricks."

"That is quite true," said the stranger. "I want more money for my rabbit than for my horse."

The townspeople gave him more money.

In great joy, they took the rabbit back to town and held him until they had an important message. They tied the message to his collar and then they waited for a quick answer. They waited for three weeks for an answer, and when the rabbit did not return during that time, they exclaimed: "We have been fooled. This rabbit is like all other rabbits. It has run away and will never come back."

The stranger's wife saw a big and angry crowd coming toward her house. "They are coming to attack you," she cried to her husband.

"Get into bed," he said. "Lie still and act as if you were dead."

When the crowd entered the house, they found the stranger wailing and crying. "Woe unto me! Woe unto me! My wife is dead!"

And then, as if he forgot something, he said, "That egg!"

Carefully, as if he were handling the most precious thing in the world, he took a jewel box out of the safe. Inside the box was an egg.

Slowly, he passed the egg several times over his wife's face, and lo and behold! his wife opened her eyes, sat up and said in a dazed tone, "What is the matter? Why is this crowd here?"

The stranger looked around and held his finger over his lips, as if to tell the crowd not to make a sound. They all walked on tip-toe and whispered among themselves.

"This is more wonderful than the rabbit."

"I should say it is," said the stranger. "I shall want more money for it."

They agreed that it was worth what the stranger asked. They paid him and they went away with the life-giving egg.

When they returned to the village, they were told that the mayor's wife was seriously sick.

"We can't do anything while she is alive. When she dies, we'll restore her life."

The mayor went around sad-looking and unhappy.

"How silly," said the townspeople. "One shouldn't worry at all. As soon as she is dead, we'll turn her back to life in a jiffy."

They begged the mayor's wife to die, but she did not like to die. Instead, she tried her best to get well.

"She may recover," said Dr. Castor Oil Magnesia.

"That is too bad," said the townspeople.

The next day, however, her fever rose and she became seriously sick. "The mayor's wife is dead!" cried the town crier. "The mayor's wife is dead!"

"That is good," cried the people, for they all loved her.

"We shall now be able to use the magic egg and give back her life to her."

They took the magic egg from the big safe and carried it in its jewel box to the mayor's house. They took out the egg with great care and slowly and carefully passed the egg once, twice, thrice over her brow. They waited for her to come back to life. She remained motionless. They passed the egg over her head thousands and thousands of times, but the mayor's wife still did not have the least bit of life in her. They kept at it for almost a week, and then someone said, "The egg is not doing her any good."

"We have been cheated," the townspeople cried.

They opened the egg and found the insides were like the insides of all other eggs.

The town's fool, who did not understand what the excitement was about, said: "Why do you say you were cheated? It looks like a good fresh egg. Let me eat it."

They gave him a pitying look, as if it would be a waste of time talking to him. They went in a crowd to find the stranger, whom they caught just as he was about to leave town. To make sure he would not escape this time, they put him in a sack.

"We'll drown him," cried the crowd.

In great anger, they carried him to the bank of a river.

"Let us find out if the water is deep enough," said one.

"Very good," said the others.

They left the stranger in the sack at the edge of the water. Then everyone went into the water with their clothing on to find out if anyone could drown in the water.

"As soon as one of us drowns," they said, "we shall know that that is a good place in which to drop the stranger."

At the water's edge, the stranger in the sack began to moan and weep.

"Who is in distress?" asked a man, passing by on the road in a buggy. He stopped the horse and buggy. "Why, someone is tied up in that sack," he said, untying the twine.

As the stranger pushed out his head, he kept saying: "I don't want to be your mayor. I don't care if the mayor is paid $50,000 a year. I don't care if I get jewels and diamonds. I don't care if everybody does pay me honor. I don't want to be your mayor."

"That sounds like a very good position," said the man who owned the buggy.

"If you think so, you may have it," said the stranger. "But I believe you should give me something in return."

"Yes, that I will. You may have my horse and buggy and this gold watch and chain."

"Get into the sack and I shall tie it up. The people will think it is you who should be their mayor."

That was done and the stranger rode off with the horse and buggy and his new watch and chain.

At last the townspeople found a good place in which to drown the stranger. It was very deep there and one of the inhabitants of Chelm had almost drowned in that spot.

They all returned to the shore. They put the sack and the man in it on a boat, and then sailed the boat into the deep part of the water, and then they threw the sack and the man into the water.

"Good riddance," they shouted. "He was a cheat and a thief and a murderer and no punishment is severe enough for him."

When they reached town, they found the stranger waiting for them. He had ridden into town, you remember, and the people had walked.

"I thought you were dead," they shouted, surprised and disappointed. "You are supposed to be dead. Why aren't you?"

"Yes. Yes," prompted the townspeople, very curious and eager to hear.

"But as soon as I was drowned and dead, I went to heaven . . ."

"Heaven!" ejaculated the people. "Heaven!"

"Yes, heaven."

"What sort of place is heaven?"

The eyes of the people were popping out and their ears were sticking out.

"It's a very nice place."

"Yes, yes," said the people.

"I don't know whether I ought to tell you after the cruel way in which you treated me."

"Please tell us," said the people, their curiosity strong within them. "You are the only person we know of who ever went to heaven."

"That's true. Maybe I should."

"Please do."

"I shall not be as cruel as you have been to me."

"We are sorry."

"Well, when I got to heaven, the angels greeted me very kindly. In fact, everybody was kind. It is true that no one works in heaven, and everybody has what he wants."

"What are you, then, doing here?" one asked him.

"It is true they wanted me to remain. But I didn't like it. You see this gold watch and chain . . ."

"Yes, yes," they said.

"They gave it to me, but I still did not like to stay."

"We cannot understand why you didn't like it. It sounds like a very nice place indeed."

"I am sure I would like such a place," said a person who was very lazy.

"So would I," said another.

"So would I," said several others.

"Why, that place is the kind of place I've always wanted. I think I'm going to the river and drown myself. I won't be so foolish as to come back from such a nice place."

Several others thought exactly the same way and they wanted to go to the river and drown themselves.

Just then the mayor came up. "What is all this tumult about?" he asked.

He was told all the wonderful tales they had heard from the stranger.

"What is this nonsense about your wanting to drown yourself? Isn't this the same man who sold you the horse that couldn't do tricks, who sold you a rabbit that couldn't run errands and who sold you the egg that couldn't help my wife?"

"Yes, yes, that's the man."

"While I am mayor, no one will drown themselves because of this rascal," shouted the mayor.

"I am sure he would not lie to us."

"It is true he might have been to heaven," said the mayor of Chelm. "I would not think of insulting him by calling him a liar. That would be too awful a thing to call even a man like that. He could manage with his trickery, but you, my good people, might not manage. And then, all of you will go to heaven someday, so why do you have to hurry."

"Our good mayor," cried the people. "He is talking sense. Why do we have to hurry? We'll be there in good time. Now let us go to eat."

But nevertheless, they held the stranger in great respect in Chelm for he was the only man they knew who had ever been to heaven and had come back with a watch and a chain.

Why to Pinsk and Not to Minsk

A CHELMITE MET ANOTHER.

"Where are you going with your baggage?"

"To Minsk."

"To Minsk?"

"Yes, to Minsk," was the answer.

When they parted, the inquiring Chelmite thought to himself: "I suspect something. I did not like the way he looked when he said he was going to Minsk. To Minsk? No. Impossible. He is going to Pinsk. Oh, yes, to Pinsk."

As he walked, he thought: "Why should he tell me he is going to Minsk when he is going to Pinsk?"

This bothered him and he could not rest. His face soon lit up. "Now I know why he says he is going to Minsk when he is going to Pinsk. He is going to Pinsk because his daughter is getting married in Pinsk and he doesn't want me to know."

He felt better. "Yes, that's it. . . . It figures. It stands to reason. It all works out so logically."

Mr. Dunkelhead
and the Horse
He Didn't Borrow

Mr. Dunklehead, the farmer, needed a horse.

"I'll borrow a horse from my neighbor," he said. "He has always been a good and kind neighbor."

As he walked the road toward his neighbor, he thought: "Suppose he says no. . . . But why should he say no? Am I not honest? Don't I pay back my debts? Am I not a religious man? Do I not do good?

"He'll lend me his horse. There is no doubt. And it is only right. Has he not borrowed from me many times? And haven't I always been glad to accommodate him?"

He now felt at ease and continued walking with firm steps.

"But if he says no. . . . But why should he say no? Haven't we always shared?"

And thus he was walking and talking to himself. Suddenly his face darkened; his steps slowed. He fancied that he had reached the house of his neighbor and he was saying to him: "Would you, my good neighbor, lend me your horse?"

In his imagination he heard his neighbor reply: "Why should I lend you my horse? All kinds of things can happen to a horse. Who knows?"

As he trudged the road, he became angrier and angrier.

"So you refuse me! You will not lend me your horse. After all I have done for you! How unkind! What an ungrateful neighbor!"

By now he had reached his neighbor's house. When he went in, as soon as he saw his neighbor, he became violent and shouted: "Who needs your horse? I can manage without your horse. Keep your horse. Who wants your horse? You can choke with it!"

When the Czar's Son
Becomes Sick

THE PEOPLE OF CHELM believe that when the Czar's son gets sick, no matter how small the sickness, no matter how teeny-weeny it may be, even if it's just a cold, he will surely die.

You ask why?

The people of Chelm know why.

They will tell you as they told me; and I am setting it down as they told it to me.

If the son of the Czar, the great and powerful ruler, should become sick, the Czarina, that is, the Czar's wife, calls a doctor like anyone else.

When the doctor arrives at the gate of the great palace, he cannot walk in; he is stopped by the guard. The doctor tells the guard why he has come.

The guard then has to seek permission from his superior to allow him to enter.

The guard first speaks to the corporal; the corporal then speaks to the sergeant; the sergeant then speaks to the second lieutenant; the second lieutenant then speaks to the first lieutenant; the first lieutenant then speaks to the major; the major then speaks to the lieutenant colonel; the lieutenant colonel then speaks to the colonel; and thus it goes, one speaking to the next higher up, until the top general is reached.

When the top general hears that the doctor is at the gate of the Czar's palace, he roars out the command: "Let the doctor enter, double quick, for the great and beloved Czar's son is sick and he needs a doctor immediately."

And the colonel will roar out the command to the lieutenant colonel: "Let the doctor enter, double quick, for our great and beloved Czar's son is sick and he needs a doctor immediately."

The lieutenant colonel will then roar out the same command, and the major will roar out the same command, and the first lieutenant will roar out the same command, and the second lieutenant will roar out the same command, and the sergeant will roar out the same command.

By now the command has reached the corporal. The corporal will roar out, louder and stronger than all the others, the same command to the private. "Let the doctor enter, double quick, for our great and beloved Czar's son is sick and he needs a doctor immediately."

On hearing this order, the private will open the massive gates, the doctor will pass through it, and then he will walk through the palace courtyard till he reaches the palace door.

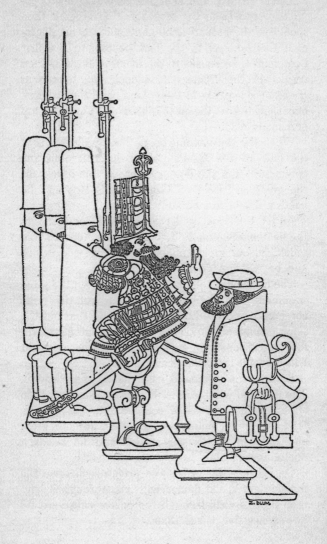

The doorman will stop the doctor and ask him what he wants.

"I am a doctor," he will explain. "The Czar's son is sick and I must go to him immediately."

In great haste, the doorman will seek out the right person in the palace so as to obtain permission to allow the doctor to enter.

"We will have to attend to this quickly," he will say. "I shall go at once to the Czar's Chamberlain."

The Czar's Chamberlain is a very important man. You cannot just walk in and see him. Before one can reach him, one has to speak to many servants and officials. And even then it is not easy, for the Chamberlain is a busy man. After seeing many servants and many officials, the doorman is now in the presence of the secretary to the Chamberlain.

"Have you an appointment with the Chamberlain?" the secretary will ask.

"No," the doorman will say.

"Then I am afraid that what you ask is impossible."

"The Czar's son is sick and the doctor is at the palace door waiting to go to him," the doorman will explain.

"Oh, that is different." The secretary now becomes very busy. "We cannot waste a minute. I shall go at once and see the Chamberlain."

When the secretary reaches the living quarters of the Chamberlain, he has to pass through a new set of servants and officials.

"There is not a moment to be lost," they will all say.

One official will quickly pass the Chamberlain's secretary on to the next official. At long last the secretary will see all the persons he has to see, and then he will rush breathlessly into the living quarters of the Chamberlain and explain why he has come.

"Oh, this is terrible," the Chamberlain will cry. "We will have to do something. My, my! The Czar's son is sick. I will rush immediately, half-dressed as I am, to see the Czar's Prime Minister."

The Chamberlain is a person of exalted rank, but in comparison to the Prime Minister he is unimportant. The Prime Minister is almost as important as the Czar, and everyone knows that there cannot be anyone greater and more important. And to reach the Prime Minister is almost as hard as reaching the Czar himself. Just imagine all the soldiers, and servants and clerks and secretaries and officials the Chamberlain will have to see and speak to before he enters the presence of the powerful Prime Minister. It is true that when the Chamberlain explains his mission everyone expedites matters, that is, everyone rushes him to the next right person to see.

The Chamberlain has now reached the Prime Minister himself who is in bed and has just been awakened.

When the Prime Minister hears the news, he cries out: "Woe is me! The Czar's son is sick. We must not lose a minute."

He dressed quickly and dashes to the quarter of the palace where the Czar lives. Since the Czar is the ruler of the whole country, you can imagine how many more soldiers, how many more officers, how many more servants, how many more guards, how many more doormen, how many more clerks, how many more secretaries, how many more officials the Prime Minister must speak to and see.

But the Prime Minister is a very important man, and everyone is eager to help him.

At last the Prime Minister hears the welcome words: "You may now enter into the presence of the exalted and the high and the mighty Czar."

Into the magnificent throne room the Prime Minister enters, bows low, and when he picks up his head, he sees first the Czarina, the wife of the Czar, her eyes red from hours of weeping.

"I am sorry I have to disturb Your Imperial Highness," says the Prime Minister to the Czar. "But the doctor has come to cure your son. He is at the palace gate. Have we your permission to admit him?"

"No, do not bother," says the Czar, sad and unhappy. "My son is dead."

"I am sorry, Your Imperial Highness," said the Prime Minister, bowing deeply, lower than before. "Isn't it always this way?"

"Yes," said the Czar, tears trickling down his face. "The doctor always comes late."

That is why in Chelm it is said that when the Czar's son has the teeniest-weeniest sickness, even a little thing like a cold, there is no use calling a doctor.

The doctor always comes late.

Chelm Captures
the Moon

CHELM LIKED THE MOON. No other town liked the moon like Chelm.

There it was up in the sky so round and silvery and bright. But the Chelm moon did not stay that way. It got smaller and smaller and then it disappeared; and the sky became black and the town was swallowed in darkness.

"If we could only keep our bright, fat, silvery moon, how nice it would be!"

They went to their Wise Men and this is what Chelm did to capture the moon.

One night they filled a big barrel of water. When they saw the full moon, round and bright, reflected in the water, they quickly, with a swift stroke, clamped a cover over the barrel.

This is how Chelm captured the moon and had it night and day.

A Road and a Hospital

In CHELM, there was a road, a very good road, that led way up, high up, into a mountain and then it came to a sudden stop and beyond was a steep precipice. When people were careless or not watchful, they would fall and they were hurt, some very badly.

Mothers warned their children to be careful, but when they became engrossed in play, they would forget, and they, too, would fall.

"This is a curse," said the people of Chelm.

They went to their Wise Men.

"You must do something," the mothers cried, "Not a single child is safe."

The Wise Men listened, stroked their long, white beards, and said: "Yes. Yes. Quite so."

"Let our Wise Men think," said the people. They tip-toed away so that there would be quiet.

Day after day, week after week, month after month, the Wise Men thought and thought.

One day all the Wise Men appeared before the people of Chelm, looking very pleased and contented with themselves.

"Our Wise Men have been working hard. They will know what to do," said the people.

And sure enough they were right.

"At the bottom of the mountain," said the wisest of the Wise Men, "we will build a hospital and when our good people fall, the doctors will be right there to take care of them."

And so it was done.

At the bottom of the terrible precipice, the people of Chelm built the biggest and finest hospital in any town, near or far.

When the hospital was finished, bright and glistening in the deep valley, the Wise Men stroked their beards vigorously, smiled contentedly, patted one another on the back in pride.

"Ah," said the people, "what other town has wise men as wise as ours?"

Do I Know Fharful!

Two strangers were riding on a train.

"From where are you?" asked one.

"From Chelm."

"From Chelm. Then you must know Fharful."

"Fharful . . . Fharful . . ." The stranger from Chelm thought long and slowly. "Fharful. . . . Such a person does not come to mind. Give me a sign."

"He is cross-eyed."

"Fharful who is cross-eyed. Such a person does not come to mind. Give me another sign."

"He has . . . how should I describe it? . . . a hunchback, a little hunchback."

"Fharful who is cross-eyed, who has a little hunchback. Such a person does not come to mind. Give me another sign."

"He limps a little on his left leg."

"Fharful who is cross-eyed, who has a little humpback, who limps a little. Such a person does not come to mind. Give me another sign."

"He never has a handkerchief, so I always think of him with a running nose."

"Fharful who is cross-eyed, who has a little humpback, who limps a little, who has a running nose. Such a person does not come to mind. Give me another sign."

"He stammers."

"Fharful who is cross-eyed, who has a little humpback, who limps a little, who has a running nose, who stammers. Such a person does not come to mind. Give me another sign."

"He has a big, hairy wart on his left cheek."

"Fharful who is cross-eyed, who has a little humpback, who limps a little, who has a running nose, who stammers, who has a hairy wart on his left cheek. Such a person does not come to mind. Give me another sign."

"He is pock-marked."

"Fharful who is cross-eyed, who has a little humpback, who limps a little, who has a running nose, who stammers, who has a hairy wart on his left cheek, who is pock-marked. Such a person does not come to mind. Give me another sign."

"I am sorry to say he is a little muddle-headed. He seems not to have the full mind he was born with. One day he came to my house, sat down at my table, looked at me sitting opposite him and said: 'What are you doing here?'"

With that the stranger from Chelm let out a shout of delight. "Fharful! Fharful! Fharful, who is cross-eyed, who has a little humpback, who limps a little, who has a running nose, who stammers, who has a hairy wart on his left cheek, who is pock-marked, who is muddle-headed. Ah, you are talking about my good friend Fharful! Fharful, a fine man, a good man, a handsome man, a smart man! Do I know Fharful!"

Who Was the Winner?

THIS WAS A BIG and wonderful day for Chelm.

On this day it was to be decided who was the most stupid child in Chelm.

Bilpy and Tilpy had won so far every test for stupidity. There were only two children left in the contest. The two children were proud and their parents were proud.

On this day one of them would win the high honor of being the most stupid child in all Chelm.

"Here is a penny for each of you," said the judges to Bilpy and Tilpy, "and with this penny buy and bring here a beautiful horse and buggy."

"Where can I buy a horse and buggy?" asked Bilpy.

"You know where—that big field where they have many horses and buggies."

"Oh, yes, yes. I do know," said Bilpy, and with

that, he dashed away, wanting to beat Tilpy and be first to bring back the horse and buggy.

Tilpy did not make a move. He laughed and laughed. He doubled up in laughter, rolling on the ground.

"Why are you laughing?"

"How stupid is Bilpy!" said Tilpy.

"Why?" asked the judges.

"He wants to buy a horse and buggy and he doesn't even know the color you want."

"Oh," said the judges. "We want a black horse and a red buggy."

Hearing that, Tilpy held firmly his penny, and he dashed off to buy a black horse and a red buggy.

Who won the contest? Who was the most stupid child in Chelm?

I did not stay for the judges' decision.

What is your guess?

Who Is Who?

"THERE IS NEVER an end to learning," said one of the Wise Men of Chelm. "They say that in Vilna there is much to learn. And I am going there to learn."

When the people of Chelm heard this, they said, "Phew. Phew. Nonsense. Others can come to learn from our Wise Men but we have nothing to learn from anyone. We know all there is to know."

Said the Wise Man: "I shall go to Vilna and see what I shall see."

When he reached Vilna, he asked: "Who is your wisest man?"

They all said the Mayor of Vilna.

"Then I shall seek him out." And he did.

When he found the Mayor of Vilna, he said: "I hear that you are a wise and learned man. I have come to learn from you."

Asked the Mayor of Vilna: "Who is my father's son, my mother's son and is not my brother?"

The Wise Man of Chelm thought and thought. Finally, he gave answers, many answers. Your cousin. Your aunt. Your niece. Your nephew. Your brother. Your sister.

The Mayor of Vilna shook his head vigorously. "No. No. No. No. No. No." He kept saying no, no, no, no, no, no, no, no, no, no, no, no until finally the Wise Man of Chelm said sadly: "I cannot guess. I do not know."

"It is I," said the Mayor of Vilna. "Yes, I."

"Ah," said the Wise Man of Chelm, "how wise! How clever! How smart!"

He could scarcely wait to get back to his own town and there tell the people what he had learned.

When he returned to Chelm, he did not waste a minute before he assembled the people in the town square.

And in truth, they were eager to hear what their Wise Man had heard and learned in Vilna.

The Wise Man of Chelm asked what the Mayor of Vilna asked, "Who is my father's son, my mother's son and is not my brother?"

The people of Chelm made one guess, another guess, another guess, and still another guess. They guessed and guessed and guessed and guessed.

The Wise Man of Chelm answered: "No. No. No. No. No. No. No. No. No. No. No. No. No. No. No. No. No." He said no so many times that he became tired of the word and changed it to "wrong, wrong, wrong, wrong, wrong, wrong, wrong, wrong, wrong."

And thus it went on, hour after hour.

Finally, the people of Chelm said: "We do not know. Please tell us."

"Are you sure?" asked the Wise Man of Chelm.

"Yes, we are too tired to go on."

It was now very late.

"It is the Mayor of Vilna," said the Wise Man of Chelm.

He looked contentedly and happily at the people, who even after being told the answer did not understand. But they hadn't gone to Vilna and they hadn't learned, as he had gone and he had learned.

Eggs and an Empty Stomach

A man asked Mr. Wimplepuff: "How many eggs can a man eat on an empty stomach?"

Mr. Wimplepuff thought hard, very hard, and very long. "Four," he said.

"Stupid," shouted his questioner. "If you ate one egg, you wouldn't have an empty stomach."

Mr. Wimplepuff laughed and laughed. He thought it was a wonderful question. "How smart and clever this man is! I'm going to look around and find someone to ask the same question."

He went from street to street and at last he found someone he knew. "Now I'll show him how smart I am," he thought.

He asked his friend: "How many eggs can a man eat on an empty stomach?"

Without hesitation, his friend answered: "One."

Mr. Wimplepuff's face fell, "If you had only said four, what a wonderful answer I would have for you," he said sadly.

Ruined by an Axe

"WE ARE ALL going to be killed, my husband, my child, and myself when this great tragedy, this great calamity will befall me."

Mrs. Fearful sobbed and wailed and moaned so loudly that her neighbors ran to find out what had happened.

They found Mrs. Fearful in the basement, but she appeared outwardly as well as you and I.

But she was inconsolable, big tears pouring from her eyes.

"What is the matter?" asked the neighbors.

"We shall all be killed. My whole family. We shall all die. My husband and my poor little child. . . ."

The neighbors begged her to explain. At last Mrs. Fearful momentarily controlled her weeping

and pointed to an axe which was embedded overhead in the ceiling.

"Why should that bother you?" asked the neighbors, mystified.

"You do not understand. You see that axe hanging from the ceiling."

"Yes, we do."

Here she renewed her howling, her groaning and her moaning. Between sobs, she explained: "Ah, my little child will come down the stairway to the basement. It will be dark and he'll fall. Then he'll scream out in pain. I shall come rushing down after him. My husband will follow me. And then we'll all be here in the basement—my child, my husband and myself—right under the axe. The axe will fall and it will hit my husband. It is a sharp axe and it will kill him instantly. It will then glance off him and hit me and it will kill me; and we shall both fall on our little child and this will kill him."

She looked upward at the axe hanging from the ceiling. Again, she burst out afresh, groaning, moaning, wailing, her whole body wrenched by sobs, the tears falling in buckets like the downpour of an April shower. "That axe will be our ruin and kill us all."

Lost Money

A BOY HAD BEEN given money to buy things at the grocery. On the way he lost the money.

Someone saw him looking for the money. "Did you lose it here?" the man asked.

"No," said the boy.

"Then why are you looking here?"

"Ah," said the boy. "Where I lost the money it is dark and here it is light."

A man lost a $20.00 bill and that is a lot of money.

He asked everyone to help him find it.

He saw a man pick up something. "Did you find my $20.00 bill?" he asked.

"No, not all of the $20.00," said the man. "I have, however, already found 60 cents of it."

More About
the Absent-Minded
Professor

As Dr. Pimplewasser, the absent-minded professor, came downstairs from the bedroom to the living room, his wife became upset and shouted: "Look at yourself!"

The absent-minded professor did not know why his wife was so angry. "I just looked at myself in the mirror while I was dressing. You see I did not forget my shoes and I did not forget my socks." He thought his wife ought to be proud of him.

"Yes, yes," said Mrs. Pimplewasser, "but look at your vests."

Professor Pimplewasser became annoyed with his wife. "You ask me to look at myself and then to look at my vest. I have looked at both. I have dressed before the mirror. How could I help but see myself and my vest?"

"You are wearing two vests, and they are of different colors. One is red and the other green."

Sure enough, the professor was wearing two vests, one red and the other green.

"You are wearing a blue suit and neither of the vests match the suit. People will laugh at you. Go upstairs and change quickly," said Mrs. Pimplewasser. "Remember you are wearing a blue suit and you should wear a blue vest."

"But we are late," said Dr. Pimplewasser. "People will be waiting for us."

Professor and Mrs. Pimplewasser were going out to visit friends.

"I know we are late," said his wife. "That is why I am so angry. But you cannot go out with two vests and both the wrong color. Go upstairs quickly and change quickly."

Professor Pimplewasser went upstairs, back to the bedroom to change.

After he was gone, Mrs. Pimplewasser waited and waited and waited and waited.

"What could have happened to him?" she thought. "It could not take all this time to take off two vests and put on his blue vest."

Finally, she went upstairs.

In the bedroom she found Professor Pimplewasser fast asleep. His clothes were neatly piled near his bed.

Mrs. Pimplewasser shook the professor and woke him up. "You were supposed to put on your blue vest and here you are asleep," she cried impatiently.

"Oh, so that was it!" said Professor Pimplewasser, rubbing his half-open eyes in astonishment. "That was why I came up. Thank you for telling me. I knew it was for something. When I started taking off my jacket and then my two vests, naturally, I thought that meant that I was ready to go to bed. So I kept taking my clothes off and then I went to bed and to sleep. And here I am," said Professor Pimplewasser, feeling very good and proud of himself that he knew where he was.

It Figures

A YOUNG MAN FROM CHELM was traveling to Pinsk to see his fiancée.

No sooner was he seated in the train than the stranger next to him said: "So you are Mottle, the son of my good friend, Zalmen, and you're going to see Rifke." The stranger scrutinized him carefully and said: "Ah, Zalmen has a fine-looking son. I'm glad for Zalmen. And Rifke will have a good husband."

The young man was mystified. "Yes, I am Zalmen's son and I'm going to Pinsk to see my fiancée, and I plan to propose to her. But how did you know all this? I have never seen you."

"Neither have I seen you, Mottle," said the stranger, "but what I told you is as plain as the nose on your face. You see that brief case you carry—the one you are holding on your lap."

"Yes, yes," said Mottle, impatiently.

"Well," said the stranger.

"Well," said Mottle.

"It's simple."

"Well, go on," said Mottle.

"Only a lawyer would carry a brief case. And I know you're from Chelm. And I think—I know Chelm a little—who in all Chelm has a son who is a lawyer? It doesn't take much thinking, for how many lawyers are there in all Chelm but one. And I know my friend, Zalmen, has a son who is a lawyer. So I know you're Mottle, Zalmen's son, the lawyer.

"And what would a young man be doing away from his work and traveling from his home on a weekday? The only such person would be a man in love. So I think. I know Pinsk much better than I do Chelm. Who would be a proper match? You could not be marrying Bebble. She is too old. Nor Sarah, her family would not be right for you; she is too low in class. So the only proper one left is Rifke. She is the right age and she is the doctor's daughter. It equals. It comes out perfectly."

"How remarkable!" said Mottle, Zalmen's son. "Unbelievable!"

The stranger shrugged his shoulders. "It's nothing. Nothing at all. It's simple, as plain as day— like the nose on your face. If one carries a brief case like you, to what other figure can one come?"

So You Changed Your Name, Too

WHILE HE WAS WALKING down the street, a man stopped him, greeted him like an old lost friend, and embraced him with affection.

"Isaac! Isaac!" the man said. "What has happened to you, Isaac? Such a long time I have not seen you. Look at yourself.

"How you have changed! You used to have a big, fine head of hair, thick like a mop. Now you have a bald head. What a change!

"Isaac, Isaac, what a man you were! You used to be strong, like an ox, with big, powerful shoulders. You remember, Isaac. I used to say: 'There goes a mighty giant.' Look at you now—small and shrunken, a nothing. Isaac, Isaac, what a change!

"And your mustache, black and big and powerful, shooting out from the sides like two pointed swords. Ah, that was a mustache! And now nothing but plain, bare skin. What a change!

"Isaac, Isaac, what has happened to you, Isaac?"

"But I'm not Isaac."

"Isaac, Isaac, so you have changed your name, too."

Laying a Floor

AFTER CHELM HAD built the outside of the school,
it had to lay floors for the classrooms.

This gave Chelm a lot of trouble.

"If we plane the wood smooth on one side, the
children will slip. If we keep the wood rough, the
children will get splinters."

Chelm did not know what to do.

They talked and discussed and argued; one said
one thing and another said another. But still they
did not know what to do. If they plane the wood
smooth on one side, the children will slip; if the
wood is kept rough, the children will get splinters.

The Wise Men knew exactly what to do. They
knew in less than a minute.

This is what they did.

They planed the wood on one side, making the surface very, very smooth, and they kept the other side rough.

And they laid it upside down.

The Wonderful, Wonderful Telegraph

Mr. Weiselhead received a letter from a cousin who lived in a faraway place.

Since Mr. Weiselhead did not know how to read, he did not know at first from whom the letter came. "Look what I got," he called out to his wife, and he showed her the letter.

"My dear cousin," his wife read. "I am sick and unable to work. My shoes are old and worn and I need a pair of new shoes badly. There are holes in the soles of them."

Mr. Weiselhead felt very badly. "My poor, dear cousin, wearing old shoes with holes! What will happen to him when it rains?"

Tears began to pour down his face.

"Why are you crying?" asked his wife.

"My poor cousin is dead."

"Dead. How terrible!"

Mrs. Weiselhead also began to cry. Finally, Mrs. Weiselhead stopped crying. "What am I doing? Where does it say in the letter that he is dead?"

"You do not understand," said her husband. "If his shoes have holes in them, his feet will get wet when it rains, and he'll catch cold, and the cold will turn to pneumonia, and he'll die."

Now Mr. and Mrs. Weiselhead both began to sob. "Our poor cousin! And he was so young. . . . We must do something."

But what to do they did not know.

Then Mrs. Weiselhead, who was the smarter of the two, said, "Let us go to our Wise Men."

"Ah, that is wise," said her husband. "They will know."

They both felt better.

"You need not worry," said one of the Wise Men of Chelm. "Wonderful things are happening. There are new inventions. Did you ever hear of the telegraph? You have to be wise and learned to know of these things; so I am not surprised that you do not know. By telegraph, you can send flowers and messages . . . why, almost anything. Send your cousin shoes by telegraph and do not waste a minute, for your cousin is in great danger."

Mr. Weiselhead went to the store and bought the strongest, nicest and most beautiful pair of shoes in all Chelm.

Mr. Weiselhead smiled slyly. That Wise Man of Chelm may be wise, but did not know how much, how very much, he, Mr. Weiselhead, really knew. Lately, they have been putting up poles and lines on the main street. Of course, they must be telegraph wires.

On one of these wires Mr. Weiselhead carefully and neatly tied his beautiful pair of new shoes. "How much better these will be than his old pair! When he receives them, I am sure my cousin will love them."

As he left, there from the wire dangled the pair of brand new shoes.

A tramp walked by and he saw the shoes. "It is exactly what I need," he thought, "a pair of brand new shoes."

He took down the new shoes, took off his old shoes and hung the old pair up; and then he walked away with a fine, solid pair of shoes.

A little while later Mr. Weiselhead came by to see what happened.

He saw the old pair of shoes dangling from the wire. "Ah, how wonderful is this invention! How marvelous! How quickly it works!" he exclaimed. "Only a few minutes ago I sent my cousin a brand new pair of shoes and here I see his old shoes. Poor man . . . he certainly needed a new pair. Look how worn are his old shoes and how big are the holes in the soles. A wonderful invention this telegraph! And how quickly it works!"

Why the Horse?

A MAN HIRED A driver to take him from Minsk to Pinsk.

The passenger mounted the wagon and the driver tugged at the reins and the horse proceeded to move.

Almost instantly they came upon a hill.

The driver said to his passenger: "I am a poor man and my horse is my only possession in all this world. If anything should happen to this horse, woe betide me! My wife and children will starve and what will happen to me?"

"I can see he is an old horse," said the passenger.

"You observe well," said the driver. "So let us both get down and walk while the horse pulls the wagon uphill."

So they did.

When they arrived at the top of the hill, the man made ready to mount the horse.

"Please don't," begged the driver. "Do you not see that the road is downhill? Do you know what may happen to a horse when he is harnessed to a wagon riding downhill? The wagon may slide or slip or get beyond control and it may crash right onto my horse and crush him. He is an old and weak horse as you can see. And I'm a poor man with no worldly possessions except this horse. Woe is me! What would I do without a horse? How would I feed my wife and children?"

"What do you want me to do?" asked the passenger.

"Let us both walk downhill. It is not as hard as walking uphill."

So they did.

Thus they walked until they came to a stretch of straight, level road. The passenger prepared to mount the wagon.

"Have mercy," pleaded the driver. "You see this is a muddy road. I do not have to tell you that on a muddy road the wheels get caught and they stick and they are hard to move. I'm a poor man. All the possessions I have in this world is this horse. Woe betide me if anything befalls this horse! Do you wish to rob my wife and children of food?"

"No. No," protested the man. "Heaven forbid!"

So they both walked beside the horse.

Since the road from Minsk to Pinsk is either uphill or downhill and the in-betweens are muddy, both passenger and driver walked all the way.

When at long last, they arrived at Pinsk, the

passenger said: "I know why I came to Pinsk. I know why you came to Pinsk. But why, I beg you, did we have to drag along this poor, old, decrepit horse?"

It's the Way You Read It

A CHELMITE WAS READING A LETTER from his son who was away from home.

"You must send me money. I need it. I cannot live on what you send me. Please send me the money immediately."

The father re-read each sentence in the letter and as he read, his tone was hard, harsh, and demanding.

"You must send me money," he read.

"The impudent rascal!" he cried. "He is ordering me around."

"I need it," he read.

"What is so strange about that? Who doesn't need money?"

He read on. "I cannot live on what you send me."

"The arrogance of the young man! Is there no limit to what he wants?"

"Please send me the money immediately."

"He orders me around. He wants me to rush right out and send him money. What impudence!"

As the father read the letter, each sentence came out like a sharp command and demand.

In great anger, he called out to his wife. "What kind of a son did you raise?"

He gave her the letter. After reading it, the mother became upset. "The poor boy! My son is in want and in desperate need."

The father was taken aback. "Where does he say that?"

"Right here in the letter. Haven't you read it?"

And she read back the letter, placing on each word such concern, such love, that it could melt the hardest heart. "You must send me money." There was pleading in her words, beseeching. "I need it. I cannot live on what you send me. Please send me the money immediately."

"Let me look at that letter again," said the husband. He, too, was now reading it beseechingly, pleadingly. "The poor boy. 'You must send me money. I need it.' Our poor boy is in want; he is desperate."

By now tears were rolling down both their faces.

"Yes, yes," said the father, "let us hurry and send him the money. Our poor son is in great need."

The Great Czar
Dresses
in the Morning

You would think it would be easy for the great Czar to get dressed.

How mistaken you are!

Consider the matter of putting on a simple piece of underwear.

When the Czar awakens in the morning in his enormous goose-feathered bed and yawns and stretches himself out full length, this is the signal for his long line of servants to file in beside his bed.

What do the servants do?

One servant takes out a piece of brand new underwear and places it on the Czar's body. No sooner does he do that than another servant takes it off and puts on another piece of underwear, a fresh piece.

And so it goes. No sooner does one servant put on a piece of clothing than another as quickly takes it off and puts on a brand-new fresh one.

And how can the great Czar ever get dressed?

The Czar and Sleep

It is simply impossible for the Czar to get any sleep.

As soon as he goes to bed, the Chamberlain shouts to the Czar's courtiers: "She . . . ee. She . . . ee. Shee . . . ee. The great Czar is sleeping. Quiet! Quiet!"

The courtiers shout to the Czar's guards: "Shee . . . ee. Shee . . . ee. She . . . ee. The great Czar is sleeping. Quiet! Quiet!"

Then the head of the guards stations a detail of soldiers near the great Czar's bedchamber. For this task he chooses men with strong and powerful voices, and they all shout at the top of their lungs: "Shee . . . ee. Shee . . . ee. Shee . . . ee. The great Czar is sleeping. Quiet! Quiet!"

They raise such a racket that no Czar can ever sleep.

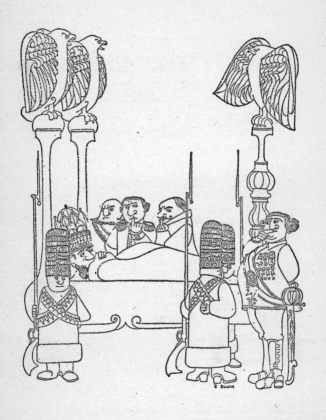

The Czar Is a Great Czar

THE CZAR IS A great Czar. He is nothing like you and me.

For instance: When you eat potatoes, you open your mouth and with a fork you yourself put the potatoes into your mouth.

Not the great Czar. No! He opens his mouth wide and a host of servants—a long line of servants, one servant after another—pitch potatoes into it . . . fast, fast, fast and faster . . ."

When you drink tea, you put the sugar into the cup of tea.

Not the great Czar. No! No!

When the great Czar drinks tea, he pours the tea into his enormously big, gold sugar bowl.

When the great Czar goes fishing, he takes with him a companion, a servant. When he reaches the water, the companion puts on a diving suit and goes to the bottom of the water with a bucket full of fish. And there at the bottom of the water with the bucket of fish, the companion waits for the great Czar's golden fishing hook to come down. When it does, the companion takes a big, fat fish out of the bucket and attaches it to the hook.

When the great Czar drops his golden fishing line into the water and then pulls it out, sure enough, and marvel to behold, every time—every single time without fail—at the end of it there is a big, fat fish.

The Czar Is the Same but Different

THE SON HAD heard many wondrous tales about the great Czar and he was talking to his father.

"They say," said the son, "that when the Czar goes into the ocean to bathe, the water becomes just right, not too hot, not too cold, just right."

"My son," said the father, "the waters of the oceans are the same for everyone, as cold for you as for the Czar. But yet when the Czar bathes, there is a Czar in the water, and it is different, for the Czar is a Czar."

"They say that when the Czar comes out of the water, he comes out dry, for he wears a miraculous bathing suit made out of awesome material."

"It is not so, my son," said the father. "You must not believe such tales. The Czar comes out of the water wet, the same as you and I. But yet when the Czar comes out of the water, it is not the same;

it is different, for he is a Czar and the Czar is a Czar."

"They say," said the son, "that when the Czar is sick all the great doctors, all the miracle workers, gather from all over the world to heal him and they are mighty and they keep the Angel of Death away from the Czar and he never dies."

"That is not so, my child. Great doctors do gather and they do stand between the Angel of Death and the Czar and they hold off the Angel of Death, but in the end the Angel of Death wins and the Czar dies as you and I and all who live will one day die. But when the Czar dies it is different, for he is a Czar and a Czar is different.

"They say, father, that the Czar does not eat what we eat."

"He eats what we eat but what he eats is different, for he is a Czar."

"Does he eat bread as we do?"

"Yes, my son, he eats bread as we do, but it is not like our bread. It is different for he is a Czar."

"Does he eat potatoes, the same potatoes that we do?"

"Yes, my son, the Czar eats potatoes as we do, but they are not like our potatoes. They are different, for he is a Czar."

"Does he eat eggs, father, as we do?"

"Yes, he eats eggs as we do, but they are not like our eggs. They are different, for he is a Czar."

"Does he drink milk, father, that a cow gives as we do?"

"Yes, he drinks milk, but it is not like our milk, for he is a Czar and the Czar is different."

"Is the Czar big, like a giant, with feet as high as a building?"

"No, no, my son. He looks like you and me, and he has the body you have—two legs, two eyes, two arms, one nose, one mouth—the same organs exactly as you have. But the Czar is different, so very different. He is a Czar, the great Czar, my son, and he is not like you and me."

The father turned to his son and said: "You understand now, my son, what a Czar is."

"Yes," said the son. "He is the same but different."

Gold and Feathers and Hope

A STRANGER CAME to Chelm and he saw many Chelmites with heads high up, holding them way up to the sky. He asked them why they walked in this strange manner and they told him this story:

To Chelm, he was told, there came a great fortune. In a far off place, there were many, many bags of gold waiting for them. To bring this great treasure to Chelm they sent many men and also their Wise Men. They wanted to make sure that nothing went wrong. Once the Chelmites had this great fortune, there would be no poor; all would have enough to eat in abundance; all would wear fine clothes; and all would live in big, luxurious houses.

As the Chelmites set out for the journey, you can imagine the excitement. They walked for hour after hour, day after day, over mountains, over deserts, through green fields and at long last they arrived at their destination. What they saw made their eyes bulge with wonder. Bags and bags and bags and bags and bags of bright, shiny gold, more gold than they ever thought there was in the world. They forgot their weariness and they laughed and they joked and their spirits were high. They did not want to waste a single minute and without resting, they began lifting the bags of gold, throwing it over their shoulders. They scarcely noticed how heavy the bags were; how they could hardly stand up under the weight. In their minds they saw what great heroes they would be when they returned to Chelm; how the mayor would greet them and how everyone would be proud of them. And the vision made them pack more and more bags of gold on their backs.

And thus they started out on their return journey. The bags of gold felt good on their backs. As they, however, walked hour after hour in the hot sun, the bags of gold became heavier and heavier. Some of the weak ones fell and even the legs of the strong ones bent.

At last, not able to bear it any longer, they cried out to their Wise Men: "You must do something."

"That is so. That is so," said the Wise Men. "We must do something."

Right there and then the Wise Men began to think fast and furiously and sure enough, one of them soon said: "I have an idea!"

"What have you?" they asked.

"An idea."

"Yes, yes," said the other Wise Men, impatiently.

They listened. "Quite right! Quite right!" they said, delighted. They felt so good that they began to pat each other on the back, proud of their own thinking.

Thereupon, they called the Chelmites together and then said: "You find it hard to carry the gold because the distances are long and your backs are weak and your feet are weary."

"Yes, yes," said the Chelmites, disappointed. "We know that. We expect better from our Wise Men."

"Patience," said the Wise Men. "You will soon see how wise we are." And then they continued. "Let us buy horses and wagons with our gold. You will still have great riches, but the riches will carry you."

"Wonderful! Wonderful!" cried the Chelmites. "How wise are our Wise Men. We will sit in our wagons and the horses will carry us. "Ah," they sighed, thinking of their tired feet, "How good that will be!"

And so it was done. In high spirits, the good Chelmites rode toward Chelm in their sturdy wagons, carried by their fine horses. Thus they went until the horses stopped and would go no further.

"We haven't given our horses food and water," said a little Chelmite, a boy.

"Yes, yes. We never thought of that. Of course, horses must eat and drink, but we have no money for food."

"Our horses will die," they cried, speaking to their Wise Men. "We are ruined. What shall we do?"

Said a Chelmite, thinking without the help of the Wise Men, "Let us sell our horses and buy food. Food is always valuable."

"Stupid! Foolish!" shouted the Wise Men. "Our valuable horses and wagons are worth great mountains of food. It will be heavier than gold. We could not carry the gold. How will we be able to carry the food? And, you must remember, gold does not spoil and food does. If we made the exchange, we will be worse off than before. We must think of something that is light."

"I have an idea," cried out one of the wisest of the Wise Men.

"Yes, yes," said all the others.

"You want something light."

"Yes, yes," they agreed.

"What is lighter than a feather?"

"Feathers. Of course!" said the Chelmites, delighted. "Why didn't we think of that before? Our Wise Men, they are truly wise."

And so it was done.

The horses and wagons were sold and with the money they bought bags and bags of feathers. The bags were so many that they filled the streets and they piled up on the tops of the roofs of the houses.

The Chelmites looked at the great mounds and mounds of feathers and they shook their heads in despair. "How can we carry such mountains and mountains of feathers?"

But the Wise Men knew what to do. You could depend on them.

A strong wind was blowing. They wet their fingers and held them up in the air. They then said: "You need not worry. You have made a good trade. This is better than horses."

"We do not understand," said the Chelmites.

"How can you understand? You are not Wise Men. Do you know in what direction the wind is blowing?"

They pointed.

"In what direction is Chelm?" the Wise Men asked.

They pointed in the same direction.

One of the Wise Men ripped open one of the bags and quickly the feathers were carried away by the wind.

"In what direction are the feathers blowing?"

"Toward Chelm," they shouted.

"Quite right. Quite right," said the Wise Men. "Why, my good people of Chelm, do you have to carry feathers to Chelm when you have God's good wind to carry them?"

"We understand. We understand," cried the Chelmites, rejoicing in their Wise Men.

Quickly they ripped open the hundreds and hundreds and hundreds and hundreds and hundreds of bags of feathers and the wind blew and blew. The sky was overcast and thick and black with feathers.

"How wonderful and how wise are our Wise Men," they said. "Look how the feathers fly away. Soon these feathers will fill the streets and the roofs of Chelm and everyone knows how valuable feathers are."

At long last, they arrived at Chelm. They did not find any feathers there. The streets were the same as always.

"What happened to the feathers?"

"What are you talking about," said the people, not understanding.

"We are ruined! We are ruined!"

They then told the people of Chelm what happened.

They all began to cry: "Our gold is gone, our horse and wagons are gone, our feathers are gone. We are ruined!"

"Stop this nonsense. Immediately! Stop it," demanded the Wise Men. "The feathers will come in good time. You saw yourself how the wind blew the feathers toward Chelm. Have patience! Have faith! What we need to do is wait and our day will come. Surely it will. One day the sky will be black with feathers and it will fall on Chelm and it will fill the town and from then on life will be soft and easy."

That's why the people of Chelm walk with heads turned upwards. Although they are very poor, they have hope that their day of great fortune will come. In truth, they are sure it will come. It is, they say, only a matter of waiting. And this hope keeps them in good spirits and also it keeps their heads high up in the sky.

Art and the
Chelm Fool

THE CZAR HAD a magnificent room whose walls were covered from floor to ceiling with four large mirrors. The Czar said to the Chamberlain: "I want four different artists to paint pictures for these walls. To the best artist I shall award a bag of gold."

The Czar's Chamberlain sent out the following command to four towns: "Send to the Czar's palace your best artist."

Chelm was one of the four towns.

When the order came, the people of Chelm said: "An artist? We have no artist, not even a bad artist. We have our work to do. We have our families. How can we leave?"

But the Chelm Fool said: "I want to go to the Czar's palace."

"You are not an artist." Because he was a fool,

the Chelmites tried to explain this to him in very simple language.

The Chelm Fool would not listen or he did not understand. He cried and cried and would not be consoled. "I want to go to the Czar's palace."

"No," said the Chelmites, "you cannot go."

The Chelm Fool became sadder and sadder. Tears would flow down his face. Everyone felt sorry for him.

Finally, one of the Wise Men said: "Our fool is as good or as bad as the best or the worst artist in Chelm. Since we have no artist, he is certainly not worse than any artist in all of Chelm. Come to think of it, I saw him make all kinds of scrawls with crayon. No one in Chelm except our fool would waste his time in this way."

This was true. Since the Chelm Fool could not learn, his teacher at school would give him crayons and he would busy himself with scribbling over sheets of paper.

"They are nothing but scrawls," said the Chelmites, "blotches that little children make who cannot write."

"Yes," said the Wise Man, "but who knows what the Czar may like."

The Chelm Fool was found in odd corners pining and sighing and he was getting thinner and sicker. "I want to go to the Czar's palace," he told anyone who would listen.

"Let him go," the Chelmites said, feeling sorry for him.

And so it was done.

The Chelm Fool set off on his journey.

At the palace, the Czar's Chamberlain accompanied the four artists to the Czar, who greeted them in his gold and jeweled throne room. "Each of you will have one wall on which to paint, and for the best picture I shall award one of you with a bag of gold."

Without wasting a moment, three of the artists set to work. They worked from morning til late at night, not stopping, day after day, week after week, month after month. They scarcely ate or slept. The fourth, the Chelm Fool, did not work. He ate in the Czar's kitchen as he never ate in his life; he played in the Czar's park, more magnificent than any he had ever seen in his life; he listened to the Czar's band, more wonderful than he had ever heard in his life. He was having a wonderful time.

Finally, the day came for the unveiling of the pictures. To this occasion came the courtiers of the Czar, dressed in their resplendent clothes, and all the great and the mighty of the land.

It was now the turn of the first artist to show his painting. As he drew the curtains apart, the assemblage gasped: "How beautiful! How beautiful!" The picture showed a shepherd and his flock of sheep near a pond in a grove of cool trees and green grass.

The next artist unveiled his picture. It was a scene of a storm-tossed coast; one could almost hear the mighty roar of the raging ocean.

"Beautiful! Very beautiful!" they all cried.

It was now the turn of the third artist and as he opened the curtain there was revealed a picture of children dancing happily to the music of an organ grinder.

"What cute children!" they all cried. "What a lovely scene!"

It was the turn of the Chelm Fool to show his painting. When he drew the curtain apart, there was a deep silence. No one spoke a word. Not a single word.

Not even the mighty Czar spoke.

The Czar came up closer. "Ah," he said, "I now see. It is a portrait. What a magnificent, kingly man! Do you observe his stature, his grace! What an elegant man! What a handsome man!"

The great men of the kingdom assembled there remained silent.

At last one of the courtiers broke the silence. "Yes, indeed, Your Imperial Majesty, what a magnificent figure!"

"Quite right," chimed in several others. "Do you not see the majesty of the man, his wisdom? How handsome he is!"

"Never have we seen the like of it," they cried in unison. "So royal! So majestic!"

At this, the Czar turned to the Chelm Fool and said: "I myself have to admit that this is a royal, elegant, and magnificent figure." He drew nearer and examined the features more closely. "We are in the presence of a great artist. I have no doubt that this picture is the best of the four."

"No doubt at all," shouted all the others.

Whereupon the great Czar, the mighty Czar, ordered his Chamberlain to award the Chelm Fool with a bag of gold. "We are proud to honor," he said, "the finest artist in our kingdom."

And this was how the Chelm Fool came back to Chelm with a bag of gold and with great honors.

"How Are Things?"...
"Half Good and Half Bad"

"HOW ARE THINGS?" asked Schmuel of his friend.

"Half good and half bad," said Jacob.

"I don't understand," said Schmuel.

"If you had my troubles," said Jacob, "you would understand."

"Let us talk about something pleasant," said Schmuel. "How is your daughter?"

Jacob's face lit up. "Is she married to a man! Nothing is too good for my daughter. A washing machine, a machine for dirty clothes, a refrigerator —the latest model ... I say to him, 'Isaac, enough is enough. My Anna has a refrigerator. After all, you work hard for your money.' He says, 'Yeh, yeh, but I want Anna to have the best, the latest model.' For Isaac nothing is too good for his wife.

"Last season was a bad season, but one day he comes home and he says to Anna, 'I bought a

187

country place.' Says Anna to Isaac, 'Why, when things are so bad do you buy a country place?' He says, 'For you, Anna, I want nothing but the best. I want you to have good fresh air to breathe, so you'll keep your cheeks nice and red. It is bad enough I have to work in a hot, dirty city in the summer; so at least you can afford to be in the country.'

"When he comes home at night from a hard day's work, he says, 'I don't want you to bother with supper. Let us go out to eat in a restaurant. Why should you sweat over a hot stove?' In the morning when he gets up, do you think he runs off to work? No, not Isaac. He first makes breakfast for the children and then for himself while my Anna—God bless her—lies in bed. And before he goes, he says to my Anna, 'You stay in bed and rest.' "

"Such a man!" said his friend Schmuel. "One in a million . . . a saint."

"That I would not say," said Jacob. "I would say that he is . . . well . . . just a husband . . . like a husband should be."

"And how is your son?" inquired Schmuel.

Jacob's face darkened. "That's my other half, my woe. My poor Morris! Is he married to a good-for-nothing who knows from nothing. How my son suffers! My heart breaks for him! Such a tragedy shouldn't even happen to an enemy. She wants and wants without a stop. She wants a dishwasher, a washing machine, a new style vacuum cleaner. Can you imagine! Such delicate hands she has. Afraid of a little soap and water . . . for what did God make hands? After my Morris comes home from a hard day's work, you would think my son is entitled to a little food, a little nourishment. You would think that a wife—a lazy good-for-nothing who is home and does nothing all day—would at least have a fine, home-cooked meal all ready on the table with a white tablecloth. She has the nerve, the gall, to say, 'Let us go to a restaurant.'

"In the morning, instead of looking after her husband who works so hard, she lies there in bed like a princess and doesn't move. And now—you wouldn't believe such a thing—she wants a country place. Is there no limit? Has she no shame? My poor boy! My poor Morris!

"So you ask why are things half good and half bad: now you understand."

Chaim and His God

Said Chaim, speaking to his God: "You are, I know, a just God and a mighty God; and you are a good bookkeeper and you keep good accounts; and for each you parcel out what is his due and what is right. Is this not so? Then, I ask, why do you not give me a little prosperity? You know how many little mouths I have to feed, my little children and my wife, who, you know, is a little tart of tongue but good of heart. Why do you keep me so hard-working and so poor that I do not know if and from where my next meal is coming, not for my children, or my wife or my self. How did you figure this to be right for me?

"Why is my lot so hard and Beril's so easy, like a tub of butter? I was just walking by Beril's house, that big house, and I looked inside and it was warm and on the table was meat enough for a feast and this is a week day; and he has no children.

"You know Beril, that low life, that scamp; he who would cheat his own mother if it would profit him.

"Are you a righteous God who does justice? Why am I not like Beril?"

As he spoke, the anger in his voice mounted.

"Me, Beril! . . . God forbid that I should be Beril, that low life, that scoundrel, not fit for man nor beast. No, good God, I do not want to be Beril or like Beril. I want to have nothing to do with him. When I think of Beril, the whole deal is off."

And thus ended Chaim's conversation with his God.

When his wife found him, his head was bowed and he appeared sad.

"You look as if you lost a fortune," she said to him.

"How right you are! I almost had it all arranged with God, and Rachel, believe me, I spoke my way right out of it."

"Ah," said his wife, sadly, "that's the reason you're Chaim and not Beril."